Crazy Hippy Gypsy

Surviving Homelessness

By
Jen Whitewing

Acknowledgements

Dedicated to my beloved son, Seth Zared Emanuel Unterseher, for putting up with me.

Love,
Mom Jen

Foreword

Jennifer Whitewing is one of the most fascinating people I have ever met. She is intelligent and wise and I thoroughly enjoy our conversations. Jen is very open about her mental illness and has taught me a great deal.

This book is written and organized as Jen assembled it. I have made very few changes to what she has done so that you can get a glimpse into how Jen thinks and what her world is like. This book may be confusing at times but welcome to her world. It's worth the journey to go along for the ride in these pages.

Jane Freund
Author, Speaker and Book Coach

Introduction and Dedication

To all my psychiatrists and counselors who helped.

I dedicate this strange autobiography to my doctors and therapists.

Dr Raskin was my mother's psychiatrist for my whole childhood. He was kind to my mother and a great help to her.

Next there was Dr. Kobe at the UW medical school. She tried but didn't help much at all. She was silent on the phone when informed of my suicide attempt on her prescribed medication.

Dr Rice was my psychiatrist at Overlake hospital for a month in Bellevue. There was a nice therapist in Athens, Georgia, named Mary Delano. She was a pro baseball player's daughter. She wore stylish floral prints. Her supervising doctor had worked at the hospital in St Louis where I stayed for a week on Arsenal street. He was enthusiastic that I had visited there. It was a bizarre week with Reggie the kleptomaniac stealing the laces out of my shoes and hiding the shoes so I couldn't leave,

In Olympia I struggled with Dr. Kookier at St Peter's mental unit and liked Dr. Cavendish.

Dr Batson was the loyal family doc for many years in Leavenworth. Dr. Wilson In Bozeman after the split from Lee. He believed me when I said I had post traumatic stress disorder and Battered Women's Syndrome.

Then red haired dashing Dr Carlson in Billings. He initiated depakote therapy and was brutally blunt about how Seth was better off with his dad than me on account of the bi-polar.

Jeanie A. MSW was one of my favorite therapists. She came into the lobby that first day with a bright floral skirt and I recall thinking, "I want her."

Back in Leavenworth I saw Dr. Olson who called me "an inspiration."

In Wenatchee and Gregg Shannon. from Harmony acupuncture. He used tuning forks and a singing crystal bowl in addition to acupuncture needles.

Now In Boise I see Dr. M. Boyer for 15 minute med checks which cost me $70! I am "Pasted together by pills." as my step father once said about my mother and she said it to me in ironic jest. I see Dr Kristina Harrington sparingly and Janet Strong NP frequently. My counselor is Heather Tustison who is pretty and kind.

Jennifer J. T. Whitewing

(The Happy Wanderer
Poor in the Land Of Plenty)
Crazy Hippie Gypsy

"Freedom's just another word for nothing left to lose." Sang Janis Joplin.

My ancestors were gypsies. Of all my family I am the darkest with the olive skin and thick curly hair of my German gypsy ancestors. I love to travel and have adventures. Being without a home, money or resources is a thrill. I like danger. This kind of living pushes you to the lunatic fringe of society.

My Father has always been a wanderer. He left his home town in Galena, Illinois and found his fortune in Alaska and the Yukon. My father met my mother in Denali National Park. They were married by a justice of the peace, with a stranger as a witness, a stranger wearing black leather who they flagged down off of his motorcycle.

After I was born there was an Earthquake. Our mobile home was destroyed and we lived with friends then lived in a one room cabin in the bush near Nebezna.

Chapter 1

By Margaret Stark White
deceased
Submitted by her daughter
Jennifer J. T. Whitewing

Good Friday Earthquake
A Mother's Story

"God if you exist, save my baby and save my life!" I prayed as I stood under my hospital room doorway during Alaska's 1964 Good Friday Earthquake, the largest earthquake in U.S. history. My daughter Jennifer had been born the day before, and I could just picture her careening around the nursery in her wheeled bed. Marriage to an atheist had caused me to doubt my own faith, but when the world rocked out from under me I turned again to God.

Finally the horrifying tumult stopped. A nurse rushed into our room.

"Girls, go to the end room and sit down. We'll bring your babies."

We sat and waited. All the babies had come except mine. I said my last name in a shaking voice, and the nurse came with Jennifer. I eagerly took her, trying to hold her, but with a new mother's awkwardness.

All the other babies were crying. Jennifer didn't move. I called a nurse, who rushed by and said, "Her color's good." Then rushed off. Jennifer still lay unmoving. Finally after five years of five minutes, she stirred in my arms. I looked down at my hand with the sapphire and diamond ring given by my great-grandmother when she survived pneumonia. That moment I promised the ring to Jennifer, as I wrote in a later poem, "promised to ache whenever you ache, promised to dance in your secret heart." Our family now calls this heirloom the survival ring.

4

Surgery patients were coming into our room because their unit had been destroyed. A nurse said gas was leaking in through open windows. Forgetting my pain, I held Jennifer on my left hip when I hurried around and closed windows.

After half an hour or so, my husband appeared to take us home. Another hospital had an emergency power unit, but our hospital staff suggested that those who could manage go home. Our trailer seven miles South of Anchorage had lost water, heat and electricity in the quake so a kind neighbor invited us into their A frame. At first we didn't know it was an earthquake. The radio mentioned possible nuclear attack, which didn't ease our minds. But then the Alaskans began to rally. Someone on the radio made a joke about a man saying, "Tell those kids to knock it off!" during the last quake. This broke our tension. Later I learned of heroics: I read of a surgeon who had lost his wife and children, doing life saving emergency surgery on others all night with tears streaming down his face. In spite of the hardship and tragedy, there was a triumph of spirit.

The next day I was sitting holding my baby. I said to my husband, "Why did we live?" The experience gave my life a sense of purpose it never had before. God had plans for me.

Joni, who was to become my close friend and Jennifer's Godmother, came by with her husband to invite us to stay in her log house further South. We made the move rather impulsively, and the living conditions were more primitive. At one point a fire started on the stove. Joni turned off the main switch and I grabbed the baby and ran outside.

"That was some quick thinking on our part." Joni said. There was no good way to rinse diapers, so I ended up using a snow bank. I practically growled at the huskies who curiously came near.

Joni and I read that babies should have a bath at ten days, so we resolutely heated some water on the Coleman stove and put a little tub near the wood barrel stove. The arching, squalling baby was nearly a match for us two inexperienced women. But we persevered, and dressed her in one of the cute pink outfits that arrived by mail from my worried relatives in the South 48. Shortly after the bath experience, all three of the other adults had gone on an errand. The house began to cool off considerably, and I worried about Jennifer getting cold. I dragged several logs in from outside and painfully lifted them into the barrel stove. I picked Jennifer up to warm her, and felt the cuddly warmth of her little body. I think it was this moment, facing the elements together, that our bonding began.

All of Alaska was boiling drinking water. I lost my milk from nervousness, which was a serious problem under the water conditions. A nurse friend recognized signs of dehydration and Jennifer was put in an incubator in the hospital for a week. We weren't able to fully establish Jennifer on a permanent formula until my mother flew in from Seattle a month after Jennifer's birth.

My mother risked her own life to come into the disaster area. I was 21, but when she greeted me at the door, she cried, "Baby!" Then, "Where's my grandchild?" My mother sustained and uplifted me through the next difficult month. She helped me keep Jennifer alive. As a result of their early bonding, my mother and Jennifer have always been extremely close.

At this point we made an overly romanticized and misguided attempt to go homesteading. We went to Nebesna, a beautiful and harsh area Northeast of Anchorage and Southeast of Fairbanks. Getting there was a saga in itself. With a truck and an old car pulling our trailer, we struggled up the highway. Vehicles kept breaking down and tires going flat.

When Jennifer cried for food, we would have to stop the car, light the Primus stove, melt snow, and finally heat the bottle. My mother remarked to Jennifer, "You are a very patient baby."

Finally we got the car and trailer within 5 miles of a remote cabin. Everyone else walked in, but Jennifer and I rode in on a dog sled. The owners of the cabin took us in, shaking their heads at our youthful rashness. They left shortly thereafter, but the rest of us stayed to battle the wilderness. The awesome white skyline at the edge of the valley, catching the light of morning and evening, was the inspiration that made us realize why we were there.

For a month in that tiny cabin there dwelled five adults, one baby a mother husky and five puppies. Needless to say tempers grew a little short under these arrangements, and it has always seemed like a miracle that Joni and I became such very close friends, keeping in touch over the years and the miles. Food was short for the adults until fortunately Joni's husband Bob shot a moose. Without that moose, we wouldn't have made it.

I was getting increasingly exhausted carrying buckets of snow and washing diapers all day. The effort in keeping Jennifer fed was enormous.

One day as I held Jennifer close, I was nearly in despair. My mother looked over at me and said, "I am someone who loves you no matter what. And that's how it'll be with Jennifer." The truth of her words echoes through the years. My mother's love gave me the extra spark I needed to keep on. My friend Joni too, though she was struggling with the situation herself, gave tireless love and support. I think now of the Footprints story: The Lord, working partly through this human love, carried me when I was too tired even to consciously pray.

My mother kept her levity, kept my spirits up. She jumped with enthusiasm when a fox ran past the window. As May sun began to hit the white spring snow, she helped me bundle Jennifer up and take her out for an airing. Jennifer's young eyes gazed up at the green cedars making dancing shadows on the snow.

Our situation did involve serious dangers. I found out later that an airplane couldn't have gotten in because of spring breakup on the muddy roads. If Jennifer or I had suffered any severe complications from the recent birth, we would have died out there. But that wasn't the plan God had for us.

After a month of this tense situation in the cabin, my father suddenly and miraculously appeared in an Alaskan friend's jeep.

"I've come to reclaim my wife." My father said, with the rather debonair poise he always exhibits under crisis. He also wanted to take Jennifer and me to Seattle for medical attention. But this possibility seemed too threatening for my husband, so I stayed with him in our cabin, trying to make a go of it in the wilderness. I cooked the rabbits he managed to shoot. A kindly neighbor brought me boiled water for the baby. My washing pans were so small I washed and hung diapers all day long. Homesteading began to seem less romantic. Finally it was too much. I bid a bittersweet goodbye to the high skyline of awesome mountains that had been my view for a month, that I hoped would be my home. We flew out and my husband put me on a plane to Seattle.

I arrived in rather the classic way at my parent's home with a baby in arms, where they took Jennifer and me in and cared for us for three and one half loving years. I found again what a rock the church could be; my church lifted me from the depths of despair.

One day my childhood sweetheart Jay came knocking on my parent's door. After a time I got an ecclesiastical annulment of my first marriage, and as Jennifer tripped up the aisle Jay and I knelt for our vows.

Today Jennifer is happily married and expecting her first baby. She wears the "survival ring" which I gave her on her 18th birthday. Our early shared hardships have made us closer over the years. My happy marriage is on its 22nd year, during which time I have been an early childhood educator, and an advocate of children nationally and internationally through my writing.

When the earth shook out from under me, and I prayed, "God if you exist..." I was really experiencing the seeds of the purpose I have found, to be a champion of children.

Chapter 2

The house in Kirkland with Peg and Bill. I remember great picture windows overlooking lake Washington and Mt. Rainier. The house would fill with the Southern sun, and the warmth of family love. On stormy days white caps would form on the lake on the crests of waves. Sitzmarck the dog was named after the mark a skier leaves in the snow when they fall. He wandered off to die. We looked for him but he never returned. Gently the cat, named because I needed to treat her gently, had kittens. They took her to the vet to get spayed and gave her kittens away while she was gone so when she returned she mewed for them and searched piteously. This greatly concerned my grandmother who had a very different policy with a later momma cat named Teanaway at Adventure Chalet.

There was a swing under the madrona tree, made with coarse rope and a smooth board my grandpa painted red. My cousins Mike and Whitney came every summer and played by the lake. We rode fast down the steep driveway on our red wagons. I set sail on my jumping Jiminy trampoline (a canvas stretched over a large tractor inner tube) and needed to be rescued by the neighbors who had a sailboat. I ate a white mushroom and showed it to my mother with a big bite out of it. She gave me syrup of epicac and I remember liking the sweet taste of it then puking and puking. Once I drove Nanny's car by releasing the brake and careening down the steep hill and through the trees. Fortunately I came to a slow stop on the grassy meadow before the lakeshore.

Grandpa Bill taught me how to climb trees safely. Together we climbed the stately evergreen pines. I would climb first with him following and reminding me to move one leg or arm at a time, "Keep three limbs on the tree." Each Christmas we would go into the woods and cut a tree.

Peggy, My mother and I lived downstairs. My grandparents Peg and Bill lived upstairs. I called my grandmother Peg "Nanny" so that the sacred term "Mommy" would be reserved for my mother. I rode down the wooden stairs on a rolled up foam mattress, bump bump bump! If I didn't get my way with my mother I'd run upstairs to see what I could get away with there.

Chapter 3

Children's story about age 3 from the point of view of a 3 year old.

The New Dad From Mercer Island

Mommy and I lived downstairs in the great house by lake Washington. Nanny and Grandad (The Old Goat or TOG) lived upstairs. My babyhood years I was happy to explore the dark pine woods, splash in the rocky lake shore and swing on the carved wooden swing under the madrona tree.

The house had been built by my grandfather. It was full of windows that looked out over the lake towards Mt. Rainier, into the woods and up the hillside where rhododendrons bloomed. The pine floors creaked slightly. The tiled bathroom had a mirrored medicine cabinet that could be opened and angled so a whole row of faces stared back from around and endless corridor.

My father was a long way away in Alaska. I remember my mother dating men who weren't my father. One had a fancy car with wings in the back. He was proud but I thought it was horrid and ran back into the house.

When Jay came into my mother's life, they fell in love and she was very happy. Jay played his Gibson guitar and gave me a tiny ukulele to play too. When Jay gave my mommy a diamond ring he gave me a ring too with tiny bells on it. He won our love, mine and mommy's.

They were married in December when I was almost four years old on a busy confusing day. I wore a pumpkin colored wool dress and carried silk and paper flowers in a shiny white basket. Two year old Mike, my cousin, saw his mother Lesley in the wedding party and started toddling up the aisle after her, crying. I clasped his hand and we marched up soberly together. Grown ups thought, "How cute." But we were very serious about it.

11

Too soon Jay, Mommy and I moved to a house on Mercer island. It was an old house with a beautiful stone fireplace, a gaping hole in the bathroom floor and large rats in the attic. I spent all the time possible outside.

Our family got a black tom kitten with white boots and Jay named him Thomas Copernicus Pounce. The rats in the attic picked on him. One rainy day Jay got mad and poisoned them. Then our house quieted and Thomas grew fat and content. Mommy got a guinea pig and I named him Torchy. "He" turned out to be a she and birthed many tiny guinea piglets. This delighted mommy, but to me they looked lifeless and hairless as they nursed off of Torchy.

Most weekends Jay's beautiful daughter Sylvia would visit. Her mommy was Katherine. We got wild. Often we'd wake on the moonlit nights
turn on the record player and dance. Then we would jump back into bed before my mommy or her daddy could catch us in the act.

Sometimes I got mad at Jay. He took up my mommy's time and didn't indulge my whims and wishes the way my grandparents did. Mommy said I was her "Only little chick." But I shared Jay with Sylvia who was two years older than I, and beautiful with blond corn silk hair.

Although I lived on Mercer island with mommy and Jay, I frequently visited Kirkland where my grandparents lived. Some weekends Sylvia and I would go to Jay's parent's house on lake Sammamish. They treated me as if I was related. I was secure that they loved me, even though Sylvia was their "real" granddaughter. There we played princesses. On Christmas we opened entirely too many presents.

Every summer my cousins Mike and Whit would visit our grandparents and see their mother Lesley. She had left them with their father. He remarried her best friend and the boys only saw their mother on vacations.
The boys and I explored the yard by the lake, towing out little red wagons. Grandma fixed our favorite foods like craft macaroni and cheese and let us add all the food coloring to the cake frosting if we wanted to, "Let's see what happens."

Sometimes when I returned to Mercer island I would cry. Jay would have to teach me the meaning of "NO" all over again. But I learned to love him because he loved my mommy. She loved him so. He tried to be a good daddy. We went on ferry boat trips to Whidbey island and played for hours on the beaches of Puget sound. I started calling Jay "Daddy."

Jay, Peggy and I moved to Mercer Island to a musty, old, rambling home with giant rats in the attic and an enchanted overgrown garden. We had a tomcat named Thomas Copernicus Pounce. He was a fighting tom, who got beat up by giant rats in our attic until we poisoned the rats. He also battled neighborhood cats.

The garden was filled with flowers. Yellow gold St. John's wort grew in the front flower bed. Overgrown yellow with pink blush roses climbed up a tree. Chamomile plants lined the gravel driveway. I nibbled on them nipping their mealy flowers. I hid for hours in the thick laurel hedges. A ravine with pear and apple trees and a creek made up the back of the property. I often climbed the holly tree and looked out toward Seattle across Lake Washington. Just down the hill was the old ferryboat dock with steep crumbling concrete.

I wrote a children's story called The Sensory Garden. It is from the point of view of a little girl playing in that garden. The little girl was me.

THE SENSORY GARDEN

The endless rain flowed in patterns down the window glass while a little girl waited for a chance to go outdoors. Her dark brown eyes watched the sky, waiting. Shafts of sun shone through the mottled gray-blue clouds. She slipped on her yellow rubber coat and matching boots and escaped the drafty, dark, old cottage into the bright freshness of the garden.

Rain soaked the earth, leaving mud puddles and tiny streams. The streams were filled with pine needles and lacy cedar twigs. She leaped over a puddle. Splash! Mud slopped around her boots, forming deep prints. A yellow and brown spotted banana slug oozed up a tree root, leaving a silver trail behind him.

The sky gradually cleared and the pure light cast hundreds of rainbows in the garden. A spider's web sagged with dew. The spider slowly incurled herself and started to repair the rips on her web. Every needle sparkled on the fir tree. The gray juniper hedge bowed, laden with water.

In the corner of the yard, in front of the cottage, a holly tree grew. The dark green shiny leaves had sharp tips. The girl slowly climbed up the slippery trunk of the holly tree, taking care not to touch the leaves. Red berries grew on the high branches. Berries were pretty but poison. She knew not to eat them. It amused her to squash them and see the white pulp and tiny seeds inside the red skin.

From her perch in the tree the view of lake Washington was amazing. Sometimes, if the wind was right, she heard the lapping of waves on the lake shore and the cries of seagulls.

Down the slippery, wet trunk of the holly tree she climbed. Over the gravel driveway she walked. Short, fragrant, yellow chamomile plants flowered in the driveway. The round flower heads tasted mealy and sweet in her mouth.

Beside the driveway was a rough wood fence. Beyond the fence was a forest of evergreen pines and cedar trees. The bark on the cedars felt like prickly cloth to her touch. Pine tree bark was bumpy with blisters of sap. She took a twig and pricked the pine tree and it squirted sticky sap onto her hand. It tasted bitter.

The girl ran away toward the ravine. She dumped the water out of an old tire swing before climbing in. She pulled herself up the muddy bank by grasping great , green bracken ferns that grew in clumps. They unfurled and grew out from the center like a fringed fan.

It was worth the hard, slick climb to swing out over the ravine and see the old orchard below. The rope creaked and stretched, twirling her around. Gnarled little apple trees and a tall pear tree grew by the brook. She scrambled down the bank to taste the fruit. Green apples were bitter, yellow apples were bland but the red apples were sweet, tart and crisp. Yellow pears were squisy and sweet. Juice ran down her chin.

Climbing out of the ravine she noticed yellow rose petals dancing in the breeze. One petal stuck on her cheek. It felt soft and silky. The dreamy smell of roses surrounded her.

The best place to hide was in the laurel hedge. Thick oval leaves and tangled trunks formed a dark green fence. Only small nimble children could pass through the maze.

From the cottage she heard her mother's voice calling her home for dinner. She wasn't hungry so she lingered for a few moments in the laurel hedge. Then she ran fast through the tall wet grass back to the cottage. With a sigh she took off her mud splattered rubber boots and rain coat. Time to go inside.

THE END

I often played outside. We lived across the street from a park with trails and swings. I tried to make my swing go all the way up and around the set.

We moved. I remember throwing all my toys, books and clothes into boxes in a jumbled disarray. We moved to Bellevue and a house with a flooded basement. Black mold crawled up the window of my bedroom. The house was full of light and had a spacious kitchen. There were weeping willows and fields of buttercups, salmonberries and a large chicken coop. It was set off at a distance from neighbor's houses. Hills of rolling unmowed and tangled grass grew. We never mowed.

Judy and Ron lived with us for a time. Judy made candles and sold pretty christals which made rainbows. Judy and Ron were studying Transcendental Meditation and practicing daily. They were a lot of fun to have around.

Chapter 4

The flooded basement held special fascination for me. It was murky and dank with a broken window and ants. One time I had a tantrum when my mother killed an ant. "Poor little ant it wanted to crawl!" I cried. I carried on for over an hour. What follows is a fictionalized story about that house and my childhood memories there. This story is for kids.

Amy's Spooky Party

Amy woke up and looked around her bedroom.

"Where's Thomas? Where's my friend?" She murmured sadly.

With a sigh Amy put on her bright orange dress. The dress was her first gift and today was Amy's tenth birthday. Mother made the warm dress and embroidered tiny pumpkins on it.

In the afternoon the girls started arriving for her party.

"Happy birthday Amy!" They said.

They came in their best party dresses and shiny shoes. They brought fancy packages of all sizes. Amy showed them around the house, careful not to open the door to the basement.

Then the girls went outside to see the chickens and the bright yellow maple trees and red vine maples.

"The leaves are turning." Amy explained.

Amy's mother called them in for cake and ice cream. The cake was chocolate swirl with fudge frosting and the ice cream was vanilla. There were ten striped pink candles on the cake.

"Make a wish!" The girls reminded Amy. Amy closed her eyes and wished for her cat Thomas to come home. He had been missing for over a week and he was such a good friend. She missed his meowing and the way he slept on the foot of her bed. Thomas would sit straight and tuck his white paws together like he was praying.

"If you talk before you finish the cake your wish will not come true." Stacy said.

Suddenly the party was no fun. If what Stacy said was true then Amy couldn't talk until she finished the huge slice of cake and the generous mound of ice cream. The other girls were chattering and giggling and didn't notice her forcing the cake and ice cream down her throat.

"What was your wish? Heather asked Amy.

"If you tell your wish then it won't come true! Stacy said with a smirk.

Amy was frozen with panic. Now she couldn't tell anyone. More than the pumpkin dress and more than the presents Amy wanted her kitty friend to return.

It was time to open the pretty presents. There were games, dolls, a paint set and stuffed animals. Everyone got party favors that un-rolled and squeaked.

After all the presents had been opened Stacy started exploring the house. She opened the door to the basement. It groaned open on rusty hinges.

"Hey Amy! What's down there?" Stacy demanded to know.

"Close that door!" Amy ordered her.

"That smells awful!" Everyone agreed.

"We're not supposed to go down there. It is flooded." Amy in-sisted.

Everyone was getting curious and nudging Amy down slimy wooden stairs that creaked.

"Let's go down. Who dares?" Stacy said.

Amy went down first followed by all the other girls. In the base-ment pools of eerie black water filled every room. Water dripped down a wall and landed with a sound like. "Drip, drop, drip, drop." Amy hesitated but the girls crowded onto the last step and she slipped and fell in. The cold water was ankle deep and muddy. Amy waded slowly over to the next room where the water was deeper. The girls silently followed in a grim procession. Spider webs caught in their hair. Their footsteps echoed on the dank stone walls. Dim light shone in from a window and cast long shadows.

Suddenly there was an awful howl coming from the rafters. The girls screamed and splashed back towards the stairs. A skinny black cat with yellow eyes perched on a rafter and his white paws glowed in the dim light.

"Oh Thomas!" Amy cried out with joy. The girls watched frozen with fear from the stairs while Amy coaxed the terrified tomcat down from a rafter.

"That is my cat. He's been missing for over a week." Amy explained to her startled friends. Thomas slowly backed down into Amy's arms. A hearty purr rattled in his throat as he clung to her with his claws.

"What's going on down there?" Mother called downstairs.

"We found Thomas!" Amy replied happily.

"Poor kitty he's been starving." The girls pointed out.

"You never should have gone down there. But you did rescue our kitty." Mother scolded them. "Just look at you! What will your mothers say?"

Quick thinking she ordered the girls to take off their muddy shoes and socks.

She rinsed out the shoes and quickly washed the socks. Then they sat around telling stories and munching on cheese popcorn while the socks tumbled in the dryer on hot. They fed watered and pet Thomas. He sat on his basket by the heater on a cedar pillow and purred so loud it rattled.

There was just a few minutes to get their socks and shoes on before their moms came to pick them up. Amy's mother didn't mention their adventure in the basement and the girls all looked like perfect tidy little ladies when their moms arrived.

At school the next day and for a long time to come Amy's spooky birthday party was a legend. The boys refused to believe it so the girls told the story again and again.

On her birthday night something scrawny, black and familiar crawled up onto Amy's bed.

"Thomas, you came home to me. My birthday wish came true!

The End

Chapter 5

I named all the chickens and we gathered eggs to eat. In the spring blue tent caterpillars would infest the willow trees and they would fall into the chicken coup and get devoured by eager chickens. This made them healthy and fertile. Little chicks were born. Lorelei was a speckled hen and my favorite. She had chicks. One fell behind the nesting box and nearly died. I rescued him and we named him Wonder. He grew to be a mighty rooster.

On my eleventh birthday I had a party with girls from my class. A neighbor boy crashed the party and brought me 11 daffodils he had picked.

We moved from the Bellevue house and I learned to stay home alone at age 11. Our cat Tarzan Balthazar disappeared when we moved and we speculated that he traveled back and forth to the old house then to the new. He was really worn out. It was a journey of 10 miles.

The Eastgate house was near a small airport. There were tiny Cesnas zooming overhead all day. As a teen I would lie with my friends at the end of the runway and watch the planes pass directly over our heads. In the livingroom hung a swinging womb chair. Jay used to call it, "The wrecking ball." Puma was a gift to me, but he loved Jay best of all. He was a beautiful Abbysinnian cat with great intelligence and savage instincts. He had to be an indoor cat as that breed isn't used to being outdoors and exposed to American cat diseases. He loved his cat pole and enjoyed chasing grapes up and down the hall. He did unspeakable indignities to the male rabbit until we got him neutered, then he calmed down considerably. Panda Bobbit Rabbit Christian was a black and white rabbit we inherited from a Christian daycare. At the time Peggy was reading the philosophy of Radichrishnan and that is why we came up with Rabbit Christian. The maple tree with a swing on it. The madrona tree. The Latvian emigrants next door who helped me to garden.

Riding my bike down the hill to Grandma Jini and grandpa Jim's house by lake Sammamish. They put in an indoor pool which was decorated with shells and plants. They had a sauna, a jaquzzi and a tanning table. The house itself overlooked Lake Sammamish with green stone floors. In the livingroom was a great book case with many old volumes including Goddey's Ladie's Book from the Victorian era. Sylvia and I used to read it to one another with mock English accents and great amusement.

At age 13 I met my biological father Jon for the first time. He was grey haired and we met him at the Greyhound bus terminal. He told me about his other kids. We spent a school day going to book stores and eating out. I listened fascinated to every word he spoke. We looked so much alike and I understood myself much better having met him. After he left my mother had a terrible mental breakdown and Jay and she put me on a bus to Leavenworth where I could be cared for by my grandparents. During this breakdown she said our house was not our house and I was not her daughter. Also she checked on me when I was sleeping to ,"Make sure I was breathing." Her doctor Dr. Raskin tried to change her medication and that only served to make matters worse. Later when I inherited my father Jon's letters I found out that my mother had an affair with Jon before her breakdown. He was cautious not to, "Get you pregnant." he promised not to to her.

At the Eastgate house we had a sad occurrence with the next door neighbors.

The new neighbors were cool, mom and I thought. A black and white couple with two little girls Chantel and Antiqua. Their dad bought them a new swing set for the back yard. Still they begged to come over to play with me. "Can we come over please pleease!" They'd beg. Their dad Chad once punished them for wanting to play with me.

At 13, I got to babysit Chantel: age 6 and Antiqua: age 8.

"Don't go into our room. Our room is off limits." Chad warned me sternly. I went in for just a moment and saw syringes, cotton, alcohol and surgical tubing. Later it made sense, the secrecy, the fear, our determination not to be prejudiced, not to see the abuse of drugs, of wife, of daughters.

Mom and I reverse discriminated. We wanted to like him because of his blackness.

Yet in time we helped his little blond wife and youngest daughter Chantelle escape over the fence. At the moment of escape it came known to us that Antiqua had to stay. Antiqua was his daughter. His possession. She was abandoned that moment by her step mother. I wondered what happened to her mother, Chad's first wife. Dead maybe?

Chad collected garbage. shot up heroin and abused his wife and girls. We drove Chantelle and her mother crouching and cowering in our car to Grandpa Jim's and Grandma Gini's house by lake Sammamish.

Chantelle splashed in the indoor pool while her mother wept and planned for their survival on the chaise lounge. The Hawaiian plants and shell lamps of the pool room made a sanctuary. She stayed the night then went to the battered women's shelter. Then she fled out of state to a relative's home. We never heard from her again.

Back home with Chad Antiqua took the pain. I called Child Protective Services. They couldn't take a report from a minor. I sobbed out the truth over the phone. CPS turned me away. My step Dad said, "Its none of our damn business." Mom went along with him.

Antiqua rarely played in the yard. One day she was called in to see the school nurse. She told her dad. He hid her for 2 weeks until her bruises healed. Another month passed. Everyone ignored the desperate situation. Except me. I couldn't rescue her.

Once again Antiqua got called in to see the nurse. This time she went into the foster care system. I never saw her again. Her father Chad returned to jail. The abuse had been worse than my 13 year old mind could imagine. She'd been raped by her own father. I never heard if she recovered.

The suburban family dream rotted. House vacant, yard overgrown. A broken swing set rusted creaking in the summer wind.

Chapter 6

Peg and Bill's home adventures. Family Adventures Incorporated was a business founded by my grandparents for taking people into the mountains and the wilderness. The Extended Family was an organization for cultural arts where everyone who came was to feel welcomed like family. The dam house in Tumwater Canyon. Near the Alps candy and gift store the house by the dam was spooky. It shook with the rush of water. It was loud with the sound of water rushing over the spillway. There were tiny mice everywhere. The scariest feature was the back porch which overhung the fish ladder. It creaked and sagged. I jumped on a rusty bare boxspring on a narrow part of the porch, daring fate. The Cashmere house by the Wenatchee river. We had an apartment upstairs across the street from the Wenatchee river. A pioneer museum set in a circle of buildings across the river fascinated me. Cashmere was a fruit growing town with grassy sagebrush on treeless mountains rising above the valley.

My grandparents loved to make the trek to the Enchantment Lakes. There the favorite encampment was Marmot Manor by lake Vivianne. A massive granite boulder in the shape of Merlin The Magician's hat provided a slight overhang under which a camp had been fashioned by the laying of stones and smoothing of dirt terraces. One high room was called the rodent room. The first and last night I spent there chipmunks ate the trail mix out of my backpack pocket. Mice dashed across my sleeping bag and even across my face as I slept. An outhouse with a view overlooked the lake from concealing evergreen hedges. A bandana marked the tree when the outhouse was occupied. A grand old larch guarded the entry to a cave where food was stored in big tins. How I loved the freeze dried strawberries! The cave was called a cashe.

Jay Creek Camp. Set up in the winter there was a huge gray tent heated by wood burning stoves. The kids sledded down the hill and onto a frozen pond in the creek. In the summer we hiked up the road to a place with beautiful rocks we called Geologist's Paradise. Then we hauled them back to camp in buckets.

8 Mile Camp: Set by the Icicle river in Icicle Canyon 8 mile camp was across the river from a large campground. In the summer there were many rock climbers scaling the granite face of 8 Mile Rock. Wool spinning and dyeing workshops were held in the big grey tent. We made sand candles by the river. There were many people living in other tents nearby. One, called the retreat tent was set far off and used for meditation and imagination trips led by my aunt Lesley.

One man had three dogs that kept tangling with a porcupine. He hunted it down and shot it. The carcass hung in a tree completely covered with yellow jackets buzzing. We ate the porcupine. It tasted fatty and delicious. Maybe the yellow jackets provided a marinade.

Adventure Chalet was a grand log home set off by itself on a hill above the Icicle river. It had been built as a bootlegger's hideout. Then after prohibition it had been a bordello, then a ski lodge and a lodge for a Catholic summer camp, and sometime in there a haunted house.

Peg and Bill rented it for very little money as it was infested with many creatures and in poor repair. There were squirrels in the attic, mice in the walls and rattle snakes in the basement. Adventure Chalet became home to Family Adventures Incorporated for over a decade. Some tents were set up on the ground. A huge grey military tent slept 40.

My first tent was emerald green and set under some shade trees facing a meadow. In it I had a table and a bean bag chair across from the bedroll. One warm summer day Lizard and I unzipped the bean bag chair to see what was inside. Intrigued we put our hands inside, then our arms. Tiny styrofoam balls clung by static to our skin. Then we put our whole heads in. Our hair was white and loaded with styrofoam beads. Laughing hysterically we got styrofoam beads everywhere. It was really a mess to clean up since we couldn't vacuum and had to sweep them up and shake the blankets. How they clung. We cleaned and repaired and furnished the chalet then built platforms in the surrounding woods and trees and put large tents on them. Everyone stayed in the tents, year round. No one slept in the chalet. I supposed that it was because it was haunted. Wood stoves kept the tents warm. Tall tarps shed the snow with a dramatic whoosh!

We built tree house tents. The first was created by a children's workshop which I took part in. Between four sturdy ponderosa pine trees we made a frame then set a plywood platform. On the platform a white canvas tent was set up with a tarp rigged above the tent so that there was a clearance of several feet. In the tent rolls of foam and canvas made a soft floor and additional rolls of foam padding made a bed. For winter warmth there was a woodburning shepherder's stove with a chimney pipe exiting the side of the tent.

In the spring kayakers came and ran the rapids in the flood swollen chilly Icicle river. Later a camp of geologists stayed for the summer. The camp was base camp for their field operations and explorations. My uncle Rowland headed the camp and brought his sons Mike and Whit. Once they caught a large rattlesnake and cooked it by simmering it in white wine and sautéing it in butter. It was wonderful to eat, although I feared rattlesnakes.

The handle on the medicine cabinet at Adventure Chalet was made of rattlesnake hide. I kind of liked the hide in a creepy way. If my grandfather killed a rattlesnake he'd get so violent with a garden hoe that he would hack it to tiny bloody bits. There was no salvaging the skin, meat or even the rattle.

Across the river and through the woods there was a Catholic Youth Organization camp called Camp Field. In the summertime the eldest lodge of campers would tromp across a temporary suspension bridge and use the upper gallery of Adventure Chalet as their dormitory. This was endlessly fascinating to my cousins and I and there were pranks and trouble all around. Once I stowed away in a trunk inside the dorm and peeked out at the boys through the keyhole. Another time I spied on them from a pine tree that got me level to their window. There was an incident when I sat in a hammock with five boys then my grandfather saw and his shadow specter scared the boys away. Once we tried to kidnap boys and one thought we were the KKK.

Best of all was when Ernie Pi drove me with one AWOL camper

from Kamiaken to the Indian caves where we enjoyed first kisses by the fire. Later we rode in the back of the truck with an engine block and Ernie weaving all over the road so we'd be thrown together.

The Chapel, made of granite and wood had awesome acoustics. I played my flute and French horn there often. Whit played his cello. Mass was casual and we often attended with grubby bare feet. I thrilled to the sound of many guitars. Other good acoustics were by the cement intake dam on the Icicle river. During winter when the irrigation ditch wasn't flowing we hiked to the tunnel and sang Gregorian chants or played instruments. A tunnel went through the solid granite mountain perfectly straight. The exit was visible from the entrance and looked like a tiny drain hole.

I went to camp at Camp Field for 2 years. It was a good experience, although I remember feeling that I didn't fit in. I learned about being one of the crowd and about Catholic traditions. One memory I have was a girl on the triple decker bunk spraying me in the face with Raid insect spray. Then I didn't get elected to their society called Order of the Cross, which made me sad. The councilors and campers voted and whoever was most popular got in. Then at the final campfire they were presented with their plastic braided leather necklace and took a vow holding a life size cross with the group. They vowed , "To protect it from the enemy, whoever he may be. And this I promise God." That's all I remember of the vow. I remember wondering if I was the enemy.

At times when I was luring male campers away from the eldest lodge at Adventure Chalet and running away with one I probably was. Or the time an elder male councilor tried to seduce me as I played my French horn in the chapel. Or the time I hid in the big old chest on the men's dorm. Or maybe when I climbed the tree next to the same dorm. It alternated boy's session then girl's session and my male cousins and I would pull similar pranks when the sex of the Kamiaken campers at the chalet dorm changed.

The preacher Father O'Grady was very kind and somewhat of an outcast himself. He had a lady in his life, which was forbidden. He died of stomach cancer after drinking himself to death. I later swore on his grave that I would never drink alcohol. That promise lasted for many years and with only a few isolated incidents of backsliding to the present day.

Adventure Chalet was a bit like a commune with many people living in the tents and sharing meals in the chalet. Chores were divided up with my grandma doing most of the cooking, cleaning and organizing. For a while folk dances happened every Friday night. My friend Elizabeth and I would trip on our bare feet trying to keep up. We danced together when men didn't ask us to dance. My Grandpa Bill would dance with us. Dancing was in the upstairs gallery and later on the outdoor dance platform we built from recycled weathered planks brought down from the irrigation ditch. The moon and starlight shone on the dancers in the cool summer evenings. I remember hiding in the boulders above the stage on the hill and watching the dancing and romancing with awe.

Kori was a black and white St. Bernard with a loving nature. He especially showed his gentle nature with kittens. He let them play on him and he watched them with concern then lavished them with a great swipe of his slobbering tongue. He was a faithful protector and companion to me and my heart broke when he got lost on Icicle ridge one dry summer day. We never found him though we searched, calling and calling.

Teanaway was a stray female momcat found by the geologists by the Teanaway river. She bore at least 12 litters of vigorous kittens, hiding them in the space above the darkroom we built in the basement. There were always kittens.

The Adventure Chalet's best friends: Dogs tend to be close friends to people, sometimes even resembling their masters in some way. Of course there were many special dogs at Adventure Chalet. Big Jim brought Baron a lab and wolf mix. Strong and fierce he has to be restrained by a chain due to his territorial nature. Older children could still play with him. Baron was known for breaking chains, big strong chains. Years later he broke loose and got hit by a freight train. It must have been a big fast train to take him down and send him to the Happy Hunting Grounds.

Candy brought a little golden bitch named Honey. She both looked like honey and acted as sweet. Her fur was fuzzy and smelled nice and fresh. She bore a litter of 6 puppies.

Ann Bard brought her kids Stevie and Suzy and they arrived with their family dog Taco. Taco was a small dog who was neither yippy nor hyper. He was enthusiastic about life and people. Taco knew how to love. He went everywhere with Stevie and Suzy, his curly black tan and white body leaping, searching and nuzzling. Once he got bit by a rattlesnake. It bit him 3 times and made him sick but didn't kill him. We were glad of this, both for the sake of the dog and the rest of us who worried about being bitten. Taco lived long, loved well until grey around the ears. Taco died and was buried at a special place on Wedge Mountain where he liked to play.

Cup Cup came to the chalet with Marlo Boyer.Both owner and dog were charming lively, popular and eccentric. Cup means foolish so Cup Cup means extremely foolish in an Indian language. He had a charming habit of leaping high into the air his small black body arched and big ears flapping. Not just once but over and over up high with a bump and scraping of toenails upon landing. One sad day at the Icicle river swim hole Marlo asked me, " Where's Kori?" And I asked him, "Where's Cup Cup?" Both dogs had recently dissapeared. We shared the pain silently for a few moments then left each without our shadow.

Kori was given to the Starks as a mature dog. He had been abused then adopted by friends who didn't have space for him. He was huge with silky curly black and white hair. He had a white ruff a white flag on the tip of his tail and ample white speckled paws.

Kori was very loving and protective of those who sought him. It was particularly endearing to see him play with the kittens. They adored him. Sometimes one would hang on to his tail so when he wagged it they flew around in the air. When they got near his mouth he'd open his huge black and pink fringed jowls and lick them from head to tail in one swipe. The drenched kitty sputtered off to the warm hearth to dry.

When he swam in the Icicle river he'd always keep his tail afloat gently waving it back and forth. I loved him more than people when I was a teenager. A friend gave me a shirt which said, "The more I know about men, the more I love my dog." This fit perfectly.

He dissapeared one hot summer day on dry Icicle ridge. We searched for him and I offered a $500 reward for his return. His loss came to us slowly, we kept hoping. Grandpa and I searched and searched hiking on the ridge. Decades later he still visits me in my dreams.

Dusty was Reed's dog. She was a lumpy fat Lab mix that had been spayed at the wrong time. She loved Kori. When she came over she would jump and run in enthusiasm for a few minutes then settle back into her sedentary ways. Kids used to tease her so she'd move. At first she'd pivot on her duff then finally roll around on her back wiggling her legs. Her face and soulful eyes resembled a seal. It took something really exciting to get her to hobble around upright. She shared my grief when Kori dissapeared.

After Kori disappeared we inherited Honey Bear who had puppies on Christmas Eve. Teanaway Kitty had kittens at the same time. The kittens nursed off of the mother dog.   She was soft, golden and very silly. Someone said she had some boxer in her. Perhaps this was why she used her front paws like hands. I remember the horrible messes in the pen by the old coal fired stove.

Later one of the pups became Stark family dog for 17 years. He was the runt with a docile spirit and a gentle, understanding way. I named him Aaron Ian. After my friend Erin and my first babysittting charge Ian. Aaron was an amazingly calm dog all black with a tiny white ruff and extra dew claws.   My mother misunderstood and thought the name was Baron Leum so Mike said the full name should be Baron Aaron Ian Von Lium Of Chalet. Pretty exalted for the runt who was a mutt!

I commented that Aaron Ian was like an emotional black body because he absorbed all incident affection. That is one of the times I said something that I'm sure impressed my grandfather Bill he laughed really hard. Black body is an object that absorbs all incident radiation.

Besides being a regular mellow rug dog Aaron Ian had bursts of enthusiasm. He dismounted from the snow cat and ran around his hind legs tucked under propelling along merrily. He ran away a few times but was always found. He lived to the ripe old age of 18 years.

Coyote didn't look like his name. He was a big fuzzzy malamute, a friend of Dan's. Hugging him was a great comfort. He was gentle and handsome with thick layers of fur that used to fill with all kinds of burrs and sticks. He resembled his curly headed bearded master. Especially when Dan wore fuzzy wool sweaters. One night Honey Bear and Coyote went out chasing chickens. Honey Bear didn't make it back. Probably she was shot. Coyote mourned more than anyone. I clung to her remaining pups and hoped. But she didn't return.

Near Adventure Chalet was an irrigation ditch filled with swift cold water. Near its oragin in Icicle cnayon was a popular hiking trail. Many tired, thirsty dogs would lean too far in for a drink and plunge downstream. They travelled for miles through granite tunnels until they reached a place where the ditch widened and slowed. That place was near the Chalet. Sometimes a dog would appear at the Chalet but most often we would hear hysterical urgent barking from up the hill. How I loved to take a leash and dogfood and hike up to meet my K-9 guest. Kori would go in the house just in case it was a territorial male dog.

One beautiful Afgan was thrilled to be rescued. She wriggled and whinned her tail whipping ectsatically. Her upset owner came for her in a few days. She seemed cruel when she loaded up her dog in the car but I could see she was loving as well. The calmest ditch lost doggy was a large labrador who probably enjoyed the swim and the extra attention that the kids lavished on him.

Once during a difficult time I dreamed that I was again at Adventure Chalet. The rooms were bare and empty of people. Everywhere there were animals; animals I'd known and animals symbolizing people who I loved. I went from room to room starting at the attic and meandering through the house to the basement where Teanaway was there with her kittens.

Kori was there. He followed me from room to room, nuzzling the baby animals, licking my ear. Even in dreams he reminds me how much I'm loved. Ten years after his dissapearance I wrote this poem:

How suprised I am to see you my dear friend. It startles me after all this time. Although I love and miss you, I try not to invoke you, yet into my dreams you appear. To lead me through metaphorical mental obstacles. To walk beside me when life is rough or painful. I wonder why, then I remember Dog spelled backwards is God.

At the chalet I remember loggerfests with log rolling in the river. Two people would try to balance on a log by rolling it either backwards or forwards in the water. The first one to fall off was the loser. Axe throwing at targets and speed log chopping were other activities. Jim our jovial giant friend excelled at axe throwing which thrilled and terrified me.

Pioneer weekends involved fleecing sheep, carding, spinning and dyeing the wool, weaving, knitting, facials with cucumbers or honey. The food was created as authentically as possible, some grew in a garden. We wore period costume.

A sauna got built in a bank overlooking the river. We would get good and hot in it then plunge in the cold Icicle river or roll in the snow.

The clinkers from the coal burning furnace surfaced the gravel parking lot. A overripe bucket of stinky slop destined for the compost heap accumulated in the kitchen. By the garden was a burn barrel for burnable trash. The ash was used for "flushing" outhouses. Most things recycled. Once there was a workshop on recycling trash into gifts.

Life at Adventure Chalet was exciting. Many people visited. People were always coming and going with tales of adventures in the mountains. Behind the Chalet was Wedge Mountain. We found many lovely wildflowers there each spring. Peg and Bill would take flower walks and help each other identify the flowers there.

We sledded down "The Big Hill" every winter, trying to bounce on our innertubes and get all the way to the smooth river ice. As a girl I tested my limits with adventures in the mountains, by the river and at Adventure Chalet. My friend Elizabeth, "Lizard" and I ran the river in inner tubes. We even took people on guided tours. I remember getting tangled up in fish weirs, rapids and eddies. The fish hatchery was one mile downstream. They built an intake dam and a diversion canal to control the water level and keep the spawning salmon where they could be harvested. We played around these structures. Once they adjusted the water level while we were downstream. We screamed and climbed trees as a two foot wall of churning brown water bore down on us and swept out inner tubes away. There was a beaver dam, ponds and several miles of isolated river. We saw a Blue Heron and sometimes eagles we saw huge half rotted and dying spawning salmon. They swam under and around us.

The canal was wide, swift and nearly straight with just one bend in it. At the end of the canal was a spillway dam, designed to prevent fish from going up the canal. It made a wonderful ice rink in the coldest part of winter. In the spring the ice would break with a thunderous roar and water would roar down the spillway. A bridge crossed the outlet of the spillway. One spring uprooted trees shot out of the boiling rapids and bashed at the bridge. I saw someone's speakers and some furniture floating by. Icicle River Island cabins upstream had flooded.

Icicle Canyon Adventure is a story I wrote for teenagers about an adventure we had in the river.

Chapter 7

Icicle Canyon Adventure

Once on a lazy warm day in August, there had been no rain for weeks and the Icicle river was drying up. Frog, Lizard and Water Rat, three teenage tomboys known to their parents as Jenny, Elizabeth and Laurie, decided to set out for an adventure.

"Let's go inner tubing," urged Frog.

"We'll bog down in the mud. I hate mud bogs." added Lizard.

"The water is so low," complained Rat.

"There's still fast whitewater in Icicle Canyon," suggested Frog, with a gleam in her brown eyes.

"We've never tried that river run through the canyon before," Rat reminded them.

"That's too dangerous!" Lizard exclaimed.

"I'm not afraid, it will be an adventure," said Frog.

"If we wear life jackets and bring extra tubes, then it might be safe," Rat reasoned.

"Let's go!" They decided their fate.

They teased their friends marc and Raymond into going along, because they drove and could drive to the launching place. On a hot day, a chilly inner tube ride sounded like a grand idea even if it was risky.

"Wear shoes. The sand burns bare feet." Marc suggested.

They took a short ride on Icicle road to the Enchantment lakes trailhead parking lot. Rock climbers and hikers looked amazed to see river runners.

"I've never seen anyone run this canyon in inner tubes," remarked a hiker. as he shouldered his backpack and started up the long trek. "Best of luck!"

"This is great!" Frog shouted as she unloaded fifteen patched inner tubes of various sizes from the back of the truck.

"This river run should be a thrill," Rat agreed.

"I can't believe we talked Marc and Raymond into coming along. They're grown ups," Lizard said. "You'd think they'd know better."

"Well girls, it's a hot day. Let's cool off in the Icicle River." Said Raymond.

"We came along to make sure you're safe," Said Marc.

All five friends stood on the bank of the river in the shade of a ponderosa pine tree and looked at the water. The flow was half it's usual level, because of the season and the lack of rain. Sparkling and clear, water swirled through the narrow canyon past grey granite boulders. In the blinding sunny heat of noonday the cold water seemed so refreshing.

Frog planned a swift mile whitewater ride down Icicle River to Adventure Chalet, where she lived. It would not take long, the water flowed so fast.

"Time to get in and go for it!" Frog said.

"Hold on tight to your inner tubes," Rat reminded everyone as they started to launch.

"Remember our motto," Lizard said. "Say it together now so the men can learn it too."

"DON'T WANNA TOUCH THE WATER!" They yelled.

Water of the Icicle River was cold enough to make muscles ache, even in August. The river flowed from mountain glaciers and melting snow. Streams cascaded down the steep canyon walls forming the river. The cold water stung so the idea was to balance on the inner tubes so that no part of the body touched the water. If, by fate one falls in for a chilly plunge, it is possible to warm up on a hot rock in the sun. Swimming very far in the Icicle River is impossible because the chill factor made muscles cramp up.

"Hold on tight! This is wild!" Frog shouted breathlessly as she launched. Deep blue green water quickly sped up as it flowed into boulders. Frog was the first adventurer into the narrow passage. The river swirled into a white froth with high waves. Before she could scream, the water flipped her over and scattered her inner tube raft out of reach.

Force of the water tumbling furiously through the rocks ripped Frog's life vest off. She flipped end over end, slamming into rocks, but she was numb to the impact because the water was so cold.

Am I going to die? Frog wondered.

The river slowed slightly and Frog came up gasping for air. Upstream the others wondered what had happened to Frog. They all managed to get out safely to shore. They saw her inner tubes and the orange life vest but no sign of Frog.

Marc and Raymond started running along the river bank, looking and calling. Frog looked at the river's edge and it seemed so far away. The cold water sapped her strength. She could barely swim. "God help me please I don't want to die!" She prayed.

Suddenly she saw a hand reaching for her. Marc's strong suntanned hand grabbed Frog's deathly cold pale hand. He pulled her to shore and dragged her to safety on a granite boulder. Frog hugged Marc, "I'm sure glad you came along, you saved me."

Frog and Marc found Raymond and walked back upstream to where Lizard and Rat were waiting. Frog warmed up and felt her cuts and bruises but was pleased that there were no broken bones.

"We worried." Rat said, while giving Frog a hug.

"I told you Icicle Canyon was too dangerous," Lizard said.

"Let's not tell our parents about this one," Frog suggested. "They may never let us run the river again. So there on the glittering sand, sparkling with fool's gold they promised one another that the misadventure would be their secret.

THE END

Chapter 8

High Camp Scottish Lakes Cross Country Ski Area: Set 11 miles off of Highway 2 on one way logging roads, this cluster of cabins were designed and constructed by my grandparents. They had no electricity and were heated by wood stoves and lighted by gas lanterns. Toilet facilities were outhouses where one flushed by dumping ashes or lye down the hole. One outhouse tent was called The Golden Castle because I said that when you peed in the snow it made an inverted "Golden Castle". It was brilliant yellow and Grandpa took a picture of me using it with my skis on and my poles holding my red mittens. It was zipped up and quite private. It was a G-rated picture.

Once a fire started in the main cabin, upstairs. The gas lamp leaked white gas and flames climbed towards the canvas tent. Bill came running down the stairs yelling, "Water! Water!" I ran upstairs with a bucket and put out the fire with two good sloshes.

Once we found evidence that a bear had broken into the upstairs of the main cabin and sat on a folding table and shot out the canvas wall into a tree where he bumped bleeding to the ground. He left impressive paw marks on the foam mattresses.

Many workers came and went, often exchanging labor for room and board and ski time. Grandpa called them YAYHOOS. The ski area was operated for the sheer joy of bringing people into the mountains. Like other retirement activities of Peg and Bill it rarely made a profit.

At first we hauled water from the creek, later implementing a gravity fed water system that even piped water through the wood stove to heat it up. The water system needed careful maintenance due to the extreme cold temperatures and periods of vacancy. It needed to be drained when we left.

The snow fell in piles up to 10 feet deep and provided excellent skiing, igloo making and snow cave digging. I practiced my French horn in a snow cave once and the snow muffled the sound completely. My cousins and I slept in a snow cave once and the warmth of our breath melted snow above our heads creatiung drips. We woke to cold water falling on our foreheads.

We used a CB radio to navigate the one way logging roads. If a logging truck was coming down loaded they couldn't stop so we needed to find a pull out and wait. It was very exciting. Once a logger heard me calling out the road numbers and letter codes and he said, "Is that a lady logger? Well alright!" This made us laugh. We rode up from the highway in the Suburban named the Blue Bird or the red snow cat (small tank) named the Thiokol or snowmobile, depending on road conditions. A few hearty souls skied all the way up. Aaron Ian, the family black lab mutt would run all the way up or down then sleep by the wood stove. I frequently skied all the way down or halfway down to Midway camp. Midway was one cabin.

The Scottish lakes were a few miles from the camp. In the summer it was a pleasant hike through the forest. In the winter it was an advanced ski through the trees. In the coldest part of winter the lakes would freeze over. I remember skiing the ridge above the lakes and looking down on them. Most of the business was in the winter although there were some guests there in the other seasons. The logging clear cuts became excellent ski slopes in the deepest snows of winter. People could cross country ski or snow shoe. There were trails and maps but no lifts or lights.

Chapter 9

The Wenatchee River home in Leavenworth was built by my grandparents Peg and Bill the year I graduated from high school. Mike and Whit tied rebar for the concrete foundation and wall. Located next to the sewage treatment plant It had no windows, except the opaque bathroom window facing that side of the house. Designed on six levels, with open shelves between the kitchen hall and living room. The upstairs got finished many years before the downstairs due to19% interest rates. The view of Edward Mesa in the Enchantment Lakes and Wedge Mountain was wonderful to the South. For many years Peg and Bill slept on the porch year round. They wore stocking caps, long warm gowns, wooly socks and brought heated hot water bottles for themselves and their dog. One feature of this house was bathrooms with two doors in them. This always made me nervous, and I'd lock both doors.

My first experience in the adult world, away from family was when I lived in Seattle in the University district house with Doug and Dan. Doug was my boyfriend and Dan was his best friend. They were Southern gentlemen from Georgia. I had what my grandmother described as a "Halcyon year." I attended Shoreline Community College in North Seattle, took Karate, studied Massage Therapy and worked at the Four Seasons Olympic Hotel.

The hotel was very lucrative and challenging as it was a four star hotel trying to become a five star hotel. Standards were exacting. I used to think of the hotel as a tiny city in microcosm, as it had its own economy, restaurants, areas of food preparation in the kitchen and ethnic segregation by department. Especially I recall the Laotian refugee stewards. Stewards were dishwashers and silver polishers. There were three restaurants: The Georgian dining room, Shuckers seafood restaurant and the Garden Court. I worked in the Garden Court as a busgirl then later as a room service waitress. I made a lot of money taking care of the super rich and spoiled people. There was a lot of ostentatious excess. I served an Arabian prince, Red Skeleton, Tom Petty and Ella Fitzgerald among others.

I felt really clear when I left that I was caring for the wrong people. I wanted to take care of poor people and people who were suffering not just people who were wealthy. After a gala party we had to throw away en entire silver bowl full of Spanish peanuts. I opened a window and tossed the nuts out onto the roof for the birds to eat. How I despised wasting food!

The house where Doug, Dan and I lived was on a steep hill and cars often backfired going down the hill. For a while we walked to the grocery store which was down the hill. There were prowlers afoot so I put up signs that said, "Beware of Rattlesnake." No one broke in.

The health food co-op was across a lush green ravine in a park. We lived upstairs in a two bedroom apartment. There was a giant mirror in the living room and a picture window overlooking the steep street.

I commuted to school by bus. My former bus driver from my days of commuting to Bellevue switched routes to the one I took to school. It was coincidence. He said, "I'm destined to be your bus driver." Named Donald Light he was kind and very helpful. When I went out at night he was protective and concerned. I recall him speaking many languages and greeting people in their own language. Later my mother told me he won Metro driver of the year.

That year I applied to Reed College and got accepted. Doug and Dan graduated from the University Of Washington. The graduation photograph they gave me was signed, "Love Eternally, Doug and Dan." But they moved. Dan went to the Peace Corps in Cameroon Africa. Doug went to work on watersheds in Juneau, Alaska. So I moved.

I went to a nice home a few blocks away on a tree lined street where I lived with strangers and worked at the hotel and kept going to karate and practicing massage therapy for free on Washington Karate Association black belts. There I fell apart. All my abandonment issues surfaced with the departure of the Southern gentlemen and my father Jon's lost promise to pay for my college tuition at Reed College.

I had a plan to swim out into Lake Washington off of Sand Point until I got hypothermia and drowned. I told this plan to my grand-parents over the phone and they convinced me to go to Harborview hospital and talk to them about it. They didn't let me leave and I stayed for one week at Harborview voluntary mental ward. There I got very co-dependant with the other patients and enjoyed a visit from my aunt Lesley and uncle Willy. The other patients and I went to a fine art museum and I found the oil paintings particularly beautiful and uplifting. It cost me a lot of my hard earned money. I remember giving massages to a lady withdrawing from heroin. She was very grateful and in a desperate panic of pain and physical and mental distress.

I tried to go back to my home with the room mates. I kept paying rent there even when I had to give up my job at the hotel and return to live with my parents in the Eastgate house. Doug and I kept in touch. He visited briefly. Then Doug moved to Georgia to attend the University of Georgia in Athens. At the last we ran out of gas in the middle of one of the floating bridges across Lake Washington while listening to Janis Joplin Take another piece of my heart... and Me and Bobbie McGee.

I registered for college in Bellevue. One course was ironically called, "Eliminating Self Defeating Behavior." There I remember meeting a boy who wanted to become a psychiatrist and giving him my book on the muscular system.

Part way through the quarter I just gave up, dropped out of school. went to my mom's home and tried to sleep all the time. Here is a poem my mother wrote at that time.

Morning Pangs

I kissed the rumpled blankets
Over your nineteen-year old form
Then looked long
At the brown tousle
That was your
Sleepy head.

The room was warm,
I felt
An illusion of safety.

I prayed,
"Please keep her
Until we meet again;"
Then it was time for work, I
Stepped outside.

I was on medication called desiprimine which proved disastrous. It made me cycle from mania to depression in one day. My mother, alarmed, called for my grandparents to come help.

I took an overdose of pills with all of them in the house and after 20 minutes told my grandmother, "Nanny I've done a very bad thing." I took all my mother's melaril and lithium, all my desiprimine and half a bottle of aspirin.

Soon the house was filled with cops and EMT's and I was on my way to Overlake hospital in an ambulance. There they pumped my stomach and I found myself numb in a room alone with white flowers from my grandparents. I stayed there for over a month. I saw One Flew Over The Cookoo's nest there and left before the last scary part where Chief smothers him.

At one point during group therapy I asked an elderly nurse, "Is there any hope?" "There is always hope she replied." I was in a deep depression. Many people came to visit me, even my step sister and her half sisters, their mother and father who were divorced came all together. It felt so odd. I felt like a judge.

Peggy visited all the time. I got into issues of abuse with the psychiatrist which set off a backlash of denial from my mom and step dad. The doctor was very concerned that I not return to their home so when I was released over a month later I moved across the country to Georgia to follow Doug, who was in graduate school at the University of Georgia at Athens.

Chapter 10

In Georgia Doug lived with room mates in a small grey house. He had one bedroom which I tried to squeeze into. The floor had a foam mattress on it on which we slept and made love. Doug was very busy and often came home late from his many activities. I worked waitress jobs. I cooked a lot of chicken breasts and rice a roni.

I recall the alpha female of the house , who played water polo had a cat named Max. Max crapped all over one carpeted room. I carefully scoured all the dried turds and tried to set up that room for doing massage therapy in. We all trauma bonded on the couch when we watched the space shuttle Challenger crash and burn. Christa McAuliffe the schoolteacher died in that crash. Soon enough things became unbearable and Doug and I moved to a three bedroom home that had been a TV Repair house made out of cinderblocks. Two fine old oak trees stood in the back yard. A grub attracting "bait bush" was found in the side yard. Black and red locusts climbed up the side of the house when it rained. Indoors bugs infested my flour, oatmeal, cornmeal and cereal. Rent was $225 per month. We rode bikes to work and school.

Doug let Denny move in to the back bedroom. Big mistake. I had a lost weekend doing sweat lodge with the Cherokee's in the woods, returned and broke up with Doug and immediately took up with Denny.

Sweat lodge was a ceremony in a small round hut with hot stones from a fire and a talking stick which was passed around in the dark. The most powerful sweat lodge was the one with 7 of us each a different race. There was a Rastaman from Jamaica, a Cherokee man from Georgia, a tall blonde man, among others and myself. We had one round for physical healing, one round for emotional healing, one round for spiritual healing and one round for the healing of the mother earth. A stick was passed between us and we could only talk when we held the stick.

Doug and Denny were friends who went to the masters program

in geography at the University of Georgia. When I sat on the hammock with Doug while breaking up with him he said to me, "Do you want to get married?" It was an afterthought proposal that only served to piss me off. Doug moved out.

I was with Denny for a while. I worked at the Stress Management clinic helping people with their chronic pain and stress in the capacity of a massage therapist. My job was wonderful. My nice boss even encouraged me to return to college. So I saved money and applied to Evergreen in Olympia, Washington.

On a trip home for the holidays I had a psychotic break on an airplane. I heard the Rush song in my head, "Fly by night away from here. Change my life again." Key issue: I didn't want to take Denny home and I wanted to get away from him. I had an intuition that he was toxic for me and the next 2 years would be cursed.

The pilot made an emergency landing in Saint Louis to let me off. A bunch of hostile cops came and dragged me off of the plane. One bashed my hand with his fist as I grasped the railing trying to hold on to the plane. I remember the full moon on the runway and the ambulance ride. Denny rode with me in the ambulance and we got taken to a nice hospital. There the social worker in the ER determined that I had no medical insurance and sent me to a old hospital on Arsenal street. There I was admitted for a week.

There I took part in a fire ceremony. Everyone begged for cigarettes from the nurses who supervised and monitored them. She gave a circle of 10 of us cigarettes and lit them one by one. It felt like we had been given the gift of fire. I don't smoke but I did then, just to fit in and to be a part of it.

There was a very dear black man who had lost his mother and girlfriend all at once and turned into a kleptomaniac. He stole my shoes so I couldn't leave. I never did locate my socks or shoe laces so I left looking like a crazy person. With a doctor's note I was allowed back on a plane, first class even. I slept the whole way on sedating medication. It was a jagged little pill called Haldol or Hell Doll as I came to think of it.

Professor's A-frame. in Athens Georgia in the woods. Denny had the right to house sit. I came to visit thinking that we were engaged. I even printed the wedding invitations. I misspelled his middle name Durban instead of Durbin and came to understand that his parents didn't approve of me and there would be no wedding. I burned the invitations one by one on the outdoor BBQ.

Overhulse house close to Evergreen where I rented a bedroom until Denny came out from Georgia.. Kira and baby Jamuna and Kira's numerous lovers coming and going. Kira wanted to be a "spoiled Greener" but she got pregnant and had to drop out. "It's the water and a lot more." Olympia beer commercial was like a joke among the many fertile women in the Olympia area.

This house was spacious and set in the woods. I had my own bedroom but was keenly aware of the traffic through Kira's bedroom.

Chapter 11

Basement apartment on Puget Sound on French Loop. We were very fortunate to live there rent free in exchange for Denny's landscape services. My favorite memory there was teaching a massage therapy workshop to my friends from Evergreen. Also dancing on the beach with my blonde friend Jennifer while the geoduck clams squirted us. It has a West view of Puget Sound. Green Thunder artillery from Fort Lewis Army Base in the distance a life foreshadowing of my new love, Lee.

White cottage in the woods. It had been Ben's home. He was gone for the summer so I moved in with. Anna (insert program from tesc)

Homeless in the woods around Evergreen State College with my German shepherd puppy and cat Joannabelle who I nicknamed Joanna Diana the Huntress when she started bringing home rabbits, snakes mice and birds.

Haunted mansion. 9 bedrooms and a model T shot up with bullet holes in the basement. The "fruit room" filled with antique purplish blue jars with old fruit preserved in them. Very pretty but unsafe to eat. I had a second story bedroom with a porch around the outside of the house. Filo and May Barrymore and a pack of 5 dogs and over 12 cats and two only children Amy and Angela one hers and one his. Lee and I visited Rainbow valley. Someone dropped LSD on Lee and we came back to the haunted mansion and he started a huge bonfire with all the firewood. Joannabelle kitty was a carrier of feline leukemia. Many of the 12 cats at the mansion died, some crawling in the attic or in the walls to fester or rot. This happened long after we moved out. The new white cow calf when I moved in Filo jumping in the trampoline to celebrate the mystery bull who swam across the Black river to mate with his cow.

Chapter 12

Tar Paper Shack. On Sleater Kinney Road in Lacey Washington the Tar Paper shack was on a ranch owned by the Dweyer family. They were a family of orphans with 8 adopted kids and also a daycare. Lee and I lived there when I was pregnant and finishing school. Joannabelle the cat disappeared so we adopted Ho Chi the booted Siamese "Temple Cat" Moses would drag Ho Chi around by the head and Ho Chi howled and curled up like a kitten. We worked for the Dweyers and helped with their ranch, pigs chickens garden and daycare. They were very kind when I was expecting, when I graduated from college and when Seth was born. We attended a sweet little church across the street. They had a potluck every Sunday. The minister said "We're the eatingest church!" Seth was the only baby born that year in that church and they held a wonderful shower with over 40 ladies present. Eight ladies pooled their money to get a safe car seat which relieved my mind. We called our home the Slave's Quarters. Seth was born in that house on September 6, 1989 at 4 in the morning. Everything went according to plan. My girlhood friend Lizard came shortly before the birth. Carmella felt that I was waiting for someone. Lizard helped heat up the little cotton hat while Lee bathed Seth in the sink. Carmella was my midwife and she was excellent. She had gentle, capable hands. Carmella was a Reike master who had attended over 1,000 births. I had no trauma, no tearing or episiotomy.

The children and their mom Jonie visited the next morning, " He's just perfect" she exclaimed. He didn't cry until he was over 10 hours old and then he cried from hunger. I nursed him and he fell contentedly asleep. We used cloth diapers and a diaper service so there would be some forests to see when he grew up.

Leavenworth house, a refuge a 6 level home on the Wenatchee river built by Peg and Bill, my grandparents. Clutter with sentimentality, traditions and hospitality for, "All God's children." as Nanny said. The Extended Family and Family Adventures Incorporated.

Chapter 13

Barmuda Triangle house. In Bozeman Montana also known as Bozoland. 7 months of hard winter. Three bars, a used clothing store, and a pizza hut all around us. "I know you're going to hate this house." Lee promised me

Moses would get loose and dash through the alleys coming home with deer sculls and moose legs crawling with vermin like fleas and mites. I went to a codependent's anonymous meeting with baby Seth and actually contemplated throwing myself down the stairs and breaking my leg just so I could be cared for. I recognized the craziness of this idea and stopped myself. I found my way to a mental health club house not far from where I lived. I gave my counselor a down baby bonnet for her baby boy. She was good but I struggled against her authority. She had me write out a contract to not harm myself and to contact her if I felt like doing so. August snowstorm destroyed our garden. All the plants turned black and wilted.

Chapter 14

Luna single wide mobile home made the same year I was born 1964. Ice box in the winter, roasting oven in the summer. We had lots of Pets and many of them including our beloved Moses died on nearby roads.

Fae Jean Dunn's farm house in Nebraska. It was a target for practicing airplanes from the nearby Air Force Base. They buzzed her home. I wondered if it was because she and her husband were veterans. I remember Fae being very emotionally supportive and sweet and taking me to her church. The sun porch where we slept. Fae Jean taking us in and feeding us well and taking us to town. Seth's grandpa Milton buying him a 5 lb. bag of raisins.

Bad break from Lee. I tried to file a Temporary Restraining Order but he beat me to it and filed one first so I couldn't go home to the trailer mobile home. I was homeless in cold Montana and winter was coming.

Chapter 15

Battered Women's Shelter was in a hidden location. It was a magical place where needs were met and emotional support was wonderful and available at all hours. Motherly and sisterly women helped one another out in a nice home with a closet that had the right size clothes for the kids and their mothers. I want to write a one act play about Thanksgiving at the shelter as it was extraordinary and the sheriff came to dinner which put us all on edge simply because he was male. He said, "I don't understand how men can beat women. Women should be protected. They are little sweeties."

Chapter 16

Eddie's house by the Crazy woman Mountains was advertised on my church bulletin board. He was going through a divorce too. Eddie was a former logger who drove dairy truck and brought home good dairy products for free. The neighbors home schooled their boy and once helped me fix my car. "Battered women always have a bum car." said Linda the shelter director. Negative divorce papers came in the mail for both Eddie and I. Seth and I shared a sunny south facing bedroom. Chickens laid fresh eggs though the extreme cold froze their combs and waddles down to nubs. We had an outdoor dog who I once rescued from the dog pound. He was a smart herding dog. One cold cold day I watched Eddie's daughter and step daughter and Seth. I kept the fire burning so the 30 below zero cold blizzarding hazardous weather wouldn't do us in. I felt so motherly and fulfilled.

Chapter 17

Rachael's apartment. A single bed in the living room. A queen size bed in a small bedroom. Rachael split from her husband the same time I separated from Lee. Her situation was very simple as there was no child custody involved. Rachael had a second story apartment in the heart of Bozeman, MT. It was sunny with natural wood and quotes from the Baha'i' Faith on the walls. Rachael once said, "Mi' casa es su casa." My house is your house. I took advantage even falling for her brother from New York who slept on a single bed in the living room. I showed him two movies: Monty Python The Meaning Of Life, and African Queen. He laughed and laughed. So many sleepovers and through depressions and manic episodes. I had no medication as I had convinced my psychiatrist that I had post traumatic stress syndrome.

One day I brought over 6 long haired chihuahuas and they leaped daintily all over the furniture. I house aped and wore out my welcome.

Chapter 18

Eric's house a vacation after Rhoda and her dogs. Eric said that long distance calls and bagels and cream cheese were "On the house". He would have had sex with me but I wasn't interested. I saw him as a father figure. His antique oriental carpet got stolen while I was there. I remember thinking how much more pain I had losing custody of my son than he had losing possession of a carpet. A tall man from Venezuela got all macho with me over something and even let my little Gizmo dog out of the yard. He got hit and the neighbors took him to the vet. He recovered OK. Brian gave the Venezuelan guy the "kiss of death" on the forehead. That ended my welcome at Eric's house. One of Eric's friends named Dharvesha said she loved it when a man ,"Stood up for his woman."

Chapter 19

Then I moved to the yellow Billings house. Seth liked it because of the nice toys in the yard. I liked it because it was a solid 3 bedroom basement apartment that was earth sheltered both cool in the summer and warm in the winter. Our upstairs neighbors were the Florez family. They were established in Billings, a second generation Mexican family with class. Jasmine played with Seth for years. Jordan was born while we lived there. Later Mr. and Mrs. Florez split up. That was rough. I shoveled the snow and Mrs. Florez hoped it was her husband. I never told her it was me. Brian liked having his own bedroom and filling it with books, sculptures and art.

Chapter 20

The doggy mobile home. Set in the tall Pines we enjoyed the double wide mobile home. The neighbors had a basset hound we nicknamed the Wienerschnitzel of Love. 8 doggies joining us for our stroll down Shore street. Shiloh cat was born on a neighboring farm.

Chapter 21

I am crazy. I have bipolar disorder or manic depressive illness. It is not something I can escape from even if I do run away from people or places. There were years in my life when I ran away and had enemies to elude. Accepting my mental illness and being "properly pilled" to quote Dr. Seuss makes me stable enough to stay in one place and maintain human relationships and fit into society.

In college I couldn't get along with my house mate. We were both only children and not used to sharing. She had 8 lovers in one month and I flipped out. I didn't want her doing "it" on my hammock. So she got me in trouble for doing bizarre things, like smashing green glass on the gravel driveway. The landlord ordered me out.

I was determined to stay in summer school. This was perilous economically since there is no financial aid for summer school. I stored everything I owned with my grandparents and kept a small orange tent, a sleeping bag and my boyfriend. My grandparents lived 160 miles away and my parents lived 70 miles away.   They were not in a position to help me out economically.

My boyfriend Lee was in the military. He kept me supplied with food. Also the woods were full of edible berries, ferns and plants. We would meet at certain places in the woods and drive places in his car. He was a supply Sargent and provided me with MRE's. Meal Ready to Eat or MRE's are tasty hearty sustenance in a bag that needs no heating or refrigeration. One soldier commented about MRE's, "They'll make a good turd."

The package makes good fire starter too. I didn't light many fires because they sent up smoke that gave away my location. Fire can keep you warm and keep the coyotes away but it can also start forest fires if not done safely.

One night at a campground a pack of coyotes came after my German Shepherd puppy and they stayed outside the fire circling and howling. We ended up sleeping on a picnic table and locking the puppy in the car so he'd be safe and the coyotes would settle down.

Another coyote encounter took place in Nisqually Delta. It is illegal to camp overnight there but we tried. We bedded down under the light of the moon. A mother coyote circled us yelping ceaselessly until we gave up and headed for the car. We thought maybe we were too close to her den. One of my magical friends said the coyote was saying: "Ha ha ha I know what you are going to have!" Meaning that we would have Seth and he'd be a coyote spirit.

At first I had my purse with I.D. and money but then I misplaced that and had no identification or money for 5 weeks. This meant no access to my meager bank account.   I couldn't afford textbooks so I found the ones I needed in the school bookstore and hid them so they wouldn't be sold. Then I proceeded to speed read and skim the texts in the book store. Also I shared books with classmates teaching myself to read upside down so we could read at the same time across the table.

The college was surrounded by miles of dense forest and many trails. I moved my camp site often so as not to be detected or leave traces of my encampment.

At The Evergreen State College there is the Free Box. People put items in to donate and others pick them up for free. Every college campus should have a free box. That summer I found some very nice clothes in the free box. Japanese exchange students came and left off silk dresses.

I wore these when I hung out at the capitol. When you are clean, well dressed and well behaved you can belong most anywhere. I met the head gardener at the capitol and got permission to gather the rose petals for potpourri. Best of all I stayed some rainy afternoons in the congressional library on their soft leather couches. For the price of juice I hung around the capitol cafeteria and read newspapers left by others.

Summer was mild with warm sunshine shining down on me through the leaves and needles of the forest I hid myself in. A strange letter came to me care of a school official. Someone 60 miles away had my purse and wanted to return it to me. It contained my student I.D. so that is how they reached me. The letter contained directions to their home. We drove for over an hour out through clear cut forests until we found a mobile home set off by itself. The people inside spilled out, giddy with relief that we weren't officials from the state or something. There an Indian man returned my purse. It had every-thing inside; cash, ID cards, address book. Nothing was missing. On the outside were skid marks. I guessed that it might have fallen off the roof of the car.

The return of my purse and the incoming financial aid of fall quarter enabled me to settle back into society and find a place to live. For a long time I was scared of being "out there" again.

Chapter 22

Fall and winter in Olympia are very rainy. I was fortunate to find a rooming house for $100 per month. The house had been built many years ago and we referred to it fondly as The Haunted Mansion. There were 9 bedrooms and a basement with an antique model T Ford car riddled with bullet holes in it. The fruit room in the basement was filled with antique canned goods that were probably dangerous to eat. There was an ample shared kitchen with home grown beef in the freezer. Two fat cows grazed in the pasture by the river. Shortly after I moved in one cow gave birth to a white calf. This was a good sign. The landlord Darryl alias Filo Barrymore celebrated the birth of the calf by jumping on a trampoline. There was a pack of dogs and 12 black cats. The king of the cats was Buster, a gnarly and grizzled battling Tom. Relieved to be settled, I retrieved Joannabelle the cat and Moses the German Shepherd dog and decorated my room with crystals, books and plants then I hung up my clothes. Fall quarter was very productive academically. I was in the Molecule To Organism program. I felt safe at the Haunted Mansion. There were two long large barns with old hay and junk. A Volkswagen bug was submerged in manure in the barn nearest the Black River.

Chapter 23

Lee and I married and we moved into a small house we called the Tar Paper Shack or the slave's quarters. It was outside of Lacey on our landlord's fine estate. There we could have our dog and cat and be near horses and 8 adopted children and a home daycare. I got pregnant right away. At the time I was not taking any medication. I remember being manic then depressed in 4 cycles during pregnancy.

We lived near St. Peter Hospital. I had been involuntarily hospitalized there 5 times the previous year. There were records of my mental illness and I felt paranoid that they would use those records against me and maybe take my baby away. Lee and I went to the hospital records office. I requested to see my records then he distracted the clerk while I took my records upstairs to a private restroom that locked. There I used a gigantic pair of very sharp shears to shred the records and flush them down the toilet. I shredded and flushed until the toilet clogged then I placed the remains wet and shredded into the bottom of a garbage can, under some paper towels. Then I took off my scarf and heavy coat and threw them away too. Lee met me and we quietly walked outside like a normal happy pregnant couple. We even took Lamaze classes at St. Peter's after that.

I graduated from college at seven months pregnant. During graduation we prayed for the students at Tianamen Square. Then I had the last trimester free to work in our garden, help in the daycare and be active in church. We attended a small church across the road where we shared our garden fresh veggies every Sunday. Our Pastor joked that we'd shake hands with the faithful then say, "Here's your zucchini." Our baby was the second born in that church community that year. The ladies were very kind and generous. They threw a baby shower attended by 40 people! I was especially pleased and relieved to receive an infant car seat.

Lee was in the military and I could have had the birth at Madigan

Army Hospital. I had my prenatal care there and found it very degrading. I was so scared of medical authority figures. So I opted for a home birth with a midwife. As a military couple we were supposed to have a nurse present but the nurse's son broke his arm the night I went into labor. So I had gentle, capable assistance from Carmella and a student midwife. My dear friend Elizabeth attended. Lee assisted and bathed Seth after he was born. It was a good birth. We found it to be a peak experience.

The day after he was born out landlady visited and said that he was just perfect. She had raised 8 but never birthed one. Her adopted kids visited and I wondered if our purpose of being at the tar paper shack was for the kids to see a family have a baby in the usual way. Moses, our German Shepherd went wild and killed a chicken on Seth's birthday. The guts spilled out and I saw all the eggs laid out from the tiny to the near fully formed. Lee beat him with the dead chicken then buried it in the garden. My placenta got buried in the garden too. Also I remember the coyotes calling in the night. A lady rode a white horse by our window. I recall thinking that Seth was a little prince or future knight being born!

When Seth was a month old we moved to Leavenworth, Washington to live with my maternal grandparents. The move was accomplished by loading 4 chickens, a Siamese cat, a German Shepherd, and Baby Seth into our Plymouth Volare and driving 160 miles. Later we loaded a rental truck with our household goods.

We had purchased an Airstream trailer that was 31 feet long. It seemed like such a cozy little home to call our own. With a screaming baby it was more like living in an echoing aluminum can. So we moved our king size waterbed into the unfinished basement and set up a crib nearby. Since I was breast feeding and since I loved him so, we slept with Seth in our bed.

My Grandparents went on a journey to The Enchantment Lakes, a trek of 10 steep miles. Lee went on a military training exercise. I was left alone in the big house with Baby Seth, a cat and two dogs. One man from the hiking party visited and expected a meal. I remember the baby crying the dogs fighting and me calling Elizabeth over to help. The soup I prepared was wickedly hot. I seasoned it with too much pepper and the man left hurriedly.

When everyone settled in it was crowded and there was much work to do. My grandparents operated a remote cross country ski resort in the Cascade mountains. Lee worked there and had jobs with the U.S. Census and a convenience store gas station called the Y-Easy Mart. I tried to do massage therapy part time in town but barely broke even. Deep memories of my own babyhood surfaced and I went into a deep depression. I resisted taking medication because I'd have to stop nursing if I did. We lived in the house in Leavenworth by the river for just under a year.

Chapter 24

Lee got accepted to the nursing school at Montana State University in Bozeman, Montana. He called me from there and told me that he had found a house that I would hate but where we could have our pets. We moved to Montana in September the week of Seth's first birthday. We lived not far from the university in a run down house that was next to the "Bar muda triangle" There were three bars and a pizza hut and a used clothing store next door. I set up a sunny nursery for Seth, but at night there were fights and breaking glass and noises so I kept him with us to keep him safe. Lee got a job right away with Godfather's pizza as a delivery man. He made good money. In the cold icy streets and blizzardy weather he earned it. School started and Lee insisted that I get a job.

I found a job at an athletic club nursery where I could bring Seth with me. It was a good job. One of the benefits was a free membership for my family. Universal Athletics Sports and Courts, Bozeman Montana. There I cared for children while their moms or dads exercised. The longest they could be left for was 2 hours. Most of the children were well cared for and Seth learned to play with kids of all ages there. The facility was beautiful, with a large play yard outside and two rooms and a bathroom. The only haunting feature was that the play yard was near a crematory and parents would think it was BBQ. I never told. Sometimes we would let the children run around in a racquetball court or in a gym. At first I walked to work or got rides with Lee. Then as it got deadly cold I feared for Seth's safety as he slept on my back. "Is he sleeping or hypothermic?" I'd wonder. So I learned to drive a car. Lee was out of town with the National Guard and I took the driving test. I failed it at the last moment by nearly getting hit by not yielding right of way. I was so upset. I had to wait a week to retake the test. My minister and his wife helped Seth and I get around until I passed my driving test at age 27!

Chapter 25

Lee found a mobile home out in the country and we moved there in the early winter. It was in a small mobile home park and it was a 1964 Luna. It was cold in the winter and hot in the summer. We had wood heat, electricity and gas and still there was frost on the inside of the walls in the bedrooms. It was near pastures with horses and cattle. We grew crops in a communal garden during the short summer growing season. The season was June through August. Bozeman had seven moths of hard winter with frost or snow. It was hard in the little single wide mobile home. We lost our beloved Moses on nearby Springhill road. He got run over by a truck. We buried him on a hill overlooking the valley. We wanted him to be some distance from the road that took his life. We made a heart of stones and placed two old pieces of wood on him, like an old rugged cross. A cat Ho Chi disappeared and our new cat Hadley got hit and died. Then our hound puppy Sally Beatrice died on the same road.

For a short time I worked at a preschool, where I brought Seth with me. It was a lovely lively little house and I "taught" 2 year olds. They were pretty rowdy and kept me hopping. Then I was recruited by a nurse to work at Massage Therapy Associates at the Holiday Inn. It was a good job where I was an independent contractor, with a client base of hotel guests and some locals. There I met Rachael, who became a dear friend.

Seasons passed in our mobile home and I left Lee. The life we had together was too hard. I had no medication for my bi-polar illness. He tried to force me to take lithium by taking Seth away. I went to the crisis center then to the Battered Women's shelter. I freaked out because of the guns in the house and my fear of Lee. I called 911. I spent one night in jail because I wouldn't cooperate with the mental health professional, and wouldn't speak without my lawyer present. The next day I secured a lawyer and got released into the battered Women's Network. I had attempted to get a restraining order, but Lee heard of it and got one against me first. So I couldn't go home. The judge ordered that I have Seth with me half of the time. This was based on my work schedule.

When I moved into the Battered Women's Shelter I found myself homeless in Montana in the fall and winter. This time I had a three year old son with me half of the time. The shelter was really nice, but there was stress and no privacy. Shelter living was a very temporary situation. The first thing I did was to invest in a sleeping bag that was good to 30 below. It was thick and had a reflective silvery lining. The bag felt like a cocoon and offered warmth, comfort and security. I sleep with it to this day.

This time I had a car. The car's name was Steve. Steve was a powerful muscle car, but unreliable. Once I got a free tow from the grocery store from some teenage boys. This was fun. Steve broke down so often and cost me so much in gas that when I did find a place to live out in the country I found that I couldn't get home due to car trouble. Once the transmission went out and the Steve died on a snowy road. Steve burned oil and had blow by. The director of the Battered Women's Shelter, Linda, said that most battered women have a bum car.

I was not sure of what to do to maintain the car. That had been the job of my ex. At one point I befriended a gas station attendant. He filled all my fluids and told me all about his life in Montana as a member of the cult Church Universal and Triumphant.

There he had been kept a virtual slave by the doomsday cult. They worked or chanted and prayed 16 hours a day, 7 days a week and couldn't leave. Only those with money were allowed to hold positions of authority or leadership in the cult. I listened to his stories as he checked my car and advised me on how to care for it.

Fortunately, during this time, I had a friend Rachael with a tiny cozy apartment in town. There I stayed with my lover (my friend's brother) on a twin bed in the living room. It strained our friendship. She has forgiven me now that she is my sister in law!

When I lived at the battered women's shelter it was nearly impossible to find an inexpensive place to live. So I looked for a long time before finding a room out of town. Eddie's house was large with a nice yard and a good view. He had been a logger who now drove dairy trucks. He was going through a divorce and had a daughter and a step daughter who visited. Our legal papers came and went in simultaneous ways as his wife left him and Lee and I divorced.

One very cold winter day I watched Seth and Eddie's girls when it was ten below outside and I kept the fire going and the kids entertained and fed. That day I felt satisfied and full as a mother. Eddie's little girl was the same age as Seth. When I moved out I told him, "Keep the deposit and spend it on your girls." It came to me free from the battered women's network so I gave it freely.

After Eddie's house I moved in to care for Rhoda and her son. There I lived rent free and earned 40 hours of pay plus my 2 other jobs part time; massage therapy and athletic club nursery.

Chapter 26

Rhoda

Rhoda loved her dogs. Twenty-seven of them. Caring for her and her son meant caring for her kennel as well. In the early summer mornings I'd walk across the yard to the barn where the dogs were kenneled. First I'd measure kibble into the bowls of the tiny long haired Chihuahuas then set them free in their yard after they gobbled their chow. Then I'd feed the shelties even the ones that tried to nip me and set them free in the other two yards. Then I'd feed the white long haired Akita with the sparkling black nose who lived on a chain in the front yard. After the dogs it was time to tend to pregnant Rhoda and her 3 year old son Ryan.

Before abandoning the family the husband bought an expensive red sports car. Then he drove from Montana to California. To his credit he did send money.

Rhoda's doctors ordered her on bed rest for the last trimester of her pregnancy. She could get up to the bathroom, but no more. She had a history of five late term miscarriages.

I moved into her home to help. My son was her son's age and we met at church. Ryan was a beautiful child with blonde curly locks and a gleam in his eye. Little Ryan went to daycare at first then got so violent he was expelled. He thought I had made his daddy go away. It seemed real enough to him. Dad moved out and I moved in. I was the enemy. So he was home and rebellious. He wanted his momma to get out of bed so bad he would act up just to get punished. It was a bitter scene with both of them yelling and her struggling out of bed chase him to his bedroom and paddle him with a wooden spoon.

His room was filled with thousands of toys as his mom used to have a daycare. Every toy had it's place and it overwhelmed him trying to clean up.
He once said he was scared of the toys. He also had a fascination and fear of the devil. His mother had indoctrinated him.

Once Ryan and my son were taking a bath together and they intentionally splashed most of the bath water on the floor. Ryan took a curtain rod and tried to gouge my son's eye out. His behavior was sometimes terrifying.

For three months we tried to keep everyone fed and clothed. And in the middle of that we sold dogs. Dog selling involved a shampoo, drying and brushing all the dogs that might be sold. While they were clean we kept them in the house. Some were potty trained, most were not.

People came by and bought dogs for bargain prices many having pity for Rhoda's delicate condition. Several sales were disastrous. One chihuahua died of a heart attack after less than one week in his new RV home. Another dog ran away in a field in town and the buyer wanted us to go find her for them, we couldn't and she was lost. A pair of dogs went to a family of 8 children and proved not house-broken. The busy exasperated mom yelled at me about it in the supermarket. I could only shrug and empathize.

The minister's wife had a carpet cleaning business and she came out with a crew of volunteers from the church and we moved all the furniture and deep cleaned the carpets with foam. Still Rhoda wanted certain dogs in the house and messes were made, which I cleaned up. One rickety old Chihuahua really wanted to sleep with Rhoda and he left dried turds all over her bedroom. I insisted he go outside at night so he would hide from me and we would make a game of chase with yipes and nipping.

I did the shopping for food as well as trips to K-mart for wading pools and toys, always more things. She was on welfare and Medicaid and had a way of acquiring things on sale. She had an urgent desire to get more things. Brian called her "A welfare queen."

One day as I was stocking food I found In the freezer in the garage entombed in a styrofoam box a dead fetus wrapped in plastic. It bore the address of a laboratory and I wondered if it had been autopsied there. Perfectly formed, it had frost bitten toes and fingers and was curled up in the fetal position forever resting among the frozen foods. I understood her desire to keep it and I never talked to her about it. I figured that she would bury it when the right time came.

It is so hard to let go.

In the last weeks of her pregnancy Rhoda developed gestational onset diabetes. Every food had to be measured or weighed and cooked carefully.

The visiting nurses came and went while I stayed to do the work. One praised me and I felt she wasn't seeing the whole imperfect picture.

Weekly I poop scooped the dog yards. One vicious sheltie named Ebony leaped up and bit me several times.   There was a trick with the hose where I'd wave the hose in the air and the dogs would quiet down and run away. They disliked the cold water.

When it rained the dogs would huddle in the barn or in the dog houses but not Gizmo. Gizmo was the stud of the chihuahuas and he would look through the glass, soaking wet, lifting one paw then the other begging to be let in. I adored Gizmo and Rhoda saw this and gave him to me as a gift to reward me for caring for the dogs.

One afternoon I ironed in Rhoda's room and we watched a movie. Little Ryan came in and jammed the tape in the VCR and broke it. He didn't mean to, but it was a loss to all of us. No more movies.

Close to nine months I drove Rhoda to the hospital with labor pains. She was sent home as it was not her time yet. One morning before dawn she came groaning across the house to awaken me and we rushed her to the hospital with little Ryan's babysitter meeting us in the labor room. We had an 18 mile drive to Bozeman and a slow truck would not let me pass. I got around him and escorted Rhoda into the hospital. The nurses were quite excited. They had seen the miscarriages.

One said, "Way to go Rhoda!" This time Rhoda was 10 centimeters dilated and soon gave birth to a healthy full term normal baby girl named Erin Rose.

I moved out as my job had ended, joyously. Her pregnancy had ended and she was no longer on bed rest. Also I had nothing left to give I was exhausted.

I wrote a fictionalized story about my little Gizmo. Who Rhoda gave me as a gift for caring for the dogs.

Jennifer J Whitewing

Eric's millionaire divorcee father figure who thought I was in love with him. Coat. Heated floor. Cinderella complex. Church Universal and Triumphant, bagels and free long distance calling. The Venezuelan carpet thief and Brian's kiss of death. Gizmo getting hurt. Dances of Universal Peace.

Billings oil refineries EXXON, CENEX and CONOCO troubled me with their omnipresence of wealth and environmental destruction. I did grow to appreciate Exxon as they sponsored a house for the Mace family through Mid-Yellowstone Valley Habitat For Humanity. West Mont sent me into the homes of 157 needy people of all ages and levels of infirmity. Parkview proved easier than home health care. I could walk 8 pleasant blocks to work. There was a lot of staff and LPN and RN nurses to help back us up and order us around. The patients had to follow nursing home routines., RMC They started up a Physician Assistant program and I applied with all my academic records and related recent work in the health field. The interview went well and I was accepted into a class of 26. Only 6 graduated and of those I never knew who passed their exams to become PAC's. I fell out of the running with a 2.0 which I am deeply ashamed of. RMC was a nice place although I found it a bit stifling and very conventional.

After my shattered dreams at RMC I worked a spring planting season at Volley Gayverts Nursery. What a lovely place held together by minimum wage employees, and "Gayvert's bandages". A Gayvert's bandage was how we used to fix things, piecemeal and cheaply. When wind swept across the frozen sand hills the greenhouses were warm and full of flora. I found the work meditative and returned to it for many years. Never a raise or a benefit to show though. "When you have a small business you try to do everything yourself." Shelley said. It was family run and all the wealth remained for the family. A good strong Catholic family.

At Mid-Yellowstone Valley Habitat For Humanity I served as a volunteer coordinator. We built 3 homes that season and I managed hundreds of volunteers. It was on a wing and a prayer. The manager and I were in a small office in a church basement with our desks facing each other. We made it happen. She amazed me. The whole organization moved on faith.

War Bonnet Inn was owned by Mexicans who rarely visited. There I met rough Montana cowboys, Indians, truckers and bed pissing lowlife drunks. At last I served the poor. I liked my boss Irene and put up with staff who used foul language, smoked and harassed me. Oh well. After a year they gave me a 15 cent per hour wage increase. "That's enough for a cup of coffee!" My friend Liz said. I enjoyed walking or biking to work past the sugar beet factory. ArtCraft Printers employed my husband for his whole time in Billings. There he bound books and made big money and helped support us. He saved money so we could eventually get out of Billings and move to Leavenworth and finally escape the black mould on the walls of the dank basement apartment.

Becoming a Baha'i'. At first in Billings Brian and I were associated with the spiritualist church. The Rev. Jeanie even married us on the 1st of the year outside by the Yellowstone river. It was a rough group of people to know. They didn't get along with one another and most were on welfare or single parents.

Then at the cultural fair I saw youthful dancers from the Baha'i faith. Enchanting and I could feel the love. Brian signed his card to make himself an official Baha'i. That weekend we followed the Bay Area Baha'i Youth Workshop to Bozeman to help out and to follow the spirit. "Say Allah' U' Abha." Brian said. I did and they all turned and waved as we drove off.

In the Baha'i faith I found myself surrounded by a spirit of unity and acceptance. The "friends" were like family for those difficult Billings years.

Slumming with the Florez family. The wrong side of the tracks. I had lived for 3 years in a mobile home so the cheerful yellow house looked just right. Seth commented "I want the house with the toys." The yard was filled with toys.

I guess I won out over many applicants to get the 3 bedroom apartment downstairs. Near the railroad tracks and busy State street the basement was quiet and warm in winter, cool in summer. As we accumulated more things and Brian made more art it began to feel too small.

Seth liked the little girl upstairs. She was a curly headed sweetheart who had a little brother while we lived there. They liked us as we were never late with rent in the 7 years we lived there. It sort of creeped me out toward the end as there was black mold on the bathroom walls and dust, cobwebs, a flooding refrigerator on old carpet and too much stuff accumulated.

I couldn't convince Brian to move. He didn't want to father my baby either so I ran away from home for a few months of car living and a serious mid life crisis. It cost me several thousand dollars in credit card bills but what the hell... that was less than 1 week languishing in a psych ward which is no fun. I drove from Montana to Idaho, Washington and Oregon many times. I racked up thousands of miles on the car. My girlfriend Elizabeth, who I stayed with some of the time in Oregon said, "You know that book, Women Who Run With The Wolves?" "Yeah." "Well you should read a book called Women Who Sleep With The Sheep!" During my travels I camped unauthorized in the woods and on the beach, in a hospital parking lot, in an airport, and on 3 college campuses including my alma mater Evergreen. Or was it a Dura Mater?

Shore street Leavenworth neighbors struggling with their sprinklers, flooding pasture, Principal and 1st grade teacher at Upper Valley Christian School. Comfortable light in a meadow. Good adjustment to moving into Peg and Bill's. Nice walk down a quiet dog lined street to the river. One day we picked up 8 assorted doggies on our walk. A neighbor's dog Bear liked to woof at us. Another dog we nicknamed The Bratwurst Of Love and Brian wrote a story about her.

Living in the woods

I am a nature girl, a tomboy and at home in nature. When broke and homeless I would rather be living in the wild woods than in the mean streets of a city. Food, shelter, privacy and solace can be found in the woods.

Of course there is danger from wildlife like insects, snakes, rodents and bears. Sometimes human predators can be found in the woods. Women are especially vulnerable to rapists and murderers. This is one time when it might be wise to have a guard dog. A dog can warn you when someone is coming and provide protection.

Getting around without a car

It is possible to live well without a car or at least without owning a car. I don't really like cars. To protest the prevalence of cars and their polluting effect on the planet I didn't learn to drive until I was 27 years old. Then I had a baby and it was cold hard winter in Montana. I remember walking with my son asleep on my back 2 miles to work and wondering, "Is he asleep or hypothermic?" Then it was time to conform and get a car and drive it like everyone else.

For those first 27 years I walked, rode a bicycle, carpooled, took the city bus or the Greyhound bus, rode the train or . Seattle Washington has an excellent bus system and I rode to work and back. I saved on parking, insurance, car payments etc. For a while I was able to save all my paychecks and live off of my tips from waitress jobs.

The bus ride was pleasant and sometimes I met interesting people. One special Metro bus driver named Donald Light seemed to always drive the route I took even when I moved from Bellevue to North Seattle. He spoke several languages and I remember him courteously greeting people in their native language. He was on my Christmas card list, but I moved so many times we lost track of each other. If ever I visit Seattle, I half expect him to be driving the bus I catch.

Walking is one of the best forms of exercise and can be done in any weather. Although I remember my umbrella turning inside out and falling apart in the wind once! Trudging through heavy snow or slush can be arduous.

Bicycles are faster than walking and fun. Currently I ride my bike to work except during downpours or snowy weather. Bicycles can be found second hand at garage sales or thrift shops for cheap. I ride past a sugar refining plant and have to dodge grubby sugar beets on the long sidewalk by the factory. In the summer they let weeds grow on the sidewalk and some of them have thorns. These tiny thorns puncture tires and inner tubes. Fortunately I discovered gel filled inner tubes. The gel seals the leaks and I don't end up with a flat tire. They are expensive but worth it. The other day I pulled 30 goat head thorns out of my front tire and the holes bubbled then sealed up.

Greyhound busses go to most major U.S cities. They can be crowded and the terminals are often in the rough parts of town. They are one of the cheapest and most reliable forms of transportation. Be sure to get to the terminal early and watch your bags. I've had bags stolen at bus depots. Ideally bring 2 small carry on bags only and avoid waiting for checked bags. The cross section of humanity you can meet while "Going Greyhound" could fill another book I hope to write.

Once I met a very wealthy college student whose fraternity brothers had bet him big money that he couldn't cross the country on a Greyhound bus. He had made it more than halfway when I met him in Montana. Once I rode a bus filled with infants and toddlers and their mothers, we dubbed it "the baby bus". Many people fleeing failed marriages pack up their children and "Go Greyhound."

Car living

Being homeless with a car allows more flexibility, freedom and a measure of safety. After serving with Americorps national service as a volunteer coordinator for Mid-Yellowstone Habitat For Humanity I was fortunate to try 2 months of homelessness in a Subaru station wagon. I needed a vacation and I ran away from home. It was a pleasure. I drove that car all up and down the Washington and Oregon coasts and between Montana and Washington. This time I had credit cards. Very risky to one's credit rating. Especially when the 2 months of crazy hippie gypsy living was extended to 5 months of unemployment after I came home and stayed in one place, contemplating the pile of bills and threatening letters from creditors. It was a case of, "Now that I'm depressed I'm truly sorry for what I did when I was manic." That was a quote from a New Yorker cartoon of a man apologizing to a court judge.

I slept in the car when I wasn't visiting friends and relatives or sleeping out under the stars. The car had fans, vents and a heater. It was bear proof and could be locked up in the city. The tinted windows gave me a measure of privacy.

For companionship I bought a lovely spotted Dalmatian puppy (on a charge card) and later a zany Greyhound mutt from the pound in Florence Oregon. I named the Dalmatian Millard, after Millard Fuller the founder of Habitat For Humanity. The Greyhound I named Harmony. She ran away once near the railroad tracks at my friend's home and I remember yelling, "HARMONY! HARMONY! HARMO-NY!" and my friend Lizard pointing out the irony of the sound of it.

Winter in Oregon and Washington was mild compared to Montana. It often rained but there was no snow or ice. Temperatures were warm. I stayed with my friends, keeping moving when I felt unwelcome or paranoid.

They worried about me but I wasn't a threat to myself or others therefore I wasn't insane enough to commit to a hospital.

Free hang outs drive all night and sleep in parks during the day. Or sleep in your car at rest areas. Bus stations, libraries, cheap fast food restaurants, big hotels, friends homes, alleys, train stations, public buildings, waiting rooms, hospital lobbies, rest areas, shopping malls, public parks, abandoned houses, abandoned buildings, college campuses, restrooms especially fancy hotel restrooms with sofas or nice restrooms at capitol buildings.

low cost hangouts
coffee houses, restaurants, ferry boats, front porches, health clubs, thrift stores, changing rooms in a department store, book stores, record stores, pet stores, shopping malls or stores of any kind.
obtaining food, shelter and clothing
The Salvation Army, The American Red Cross, St Vincent De Paul, Homeless shelters, battered women's shelters, military forts, college campuses
Finding a potty
Out in nature this is no problem, providing that you are alone and have paper if needed. Just dig a hole behind a tree and cover it up. Lacking paper a soft large green leaf will do. Remember it is biode-

gradable and natural. If near a trail or a well traveled area it is polite to bury your stools.

In the city finding a potty is very stressful. It is foul to urinate in alleys. I found that it is possible to use public restrooms or fast food restaurant restrooms. Just go in and act like you belong. Usually people are too busy to notice if you are buying anything. If necessary you can order the cheapest thing on the menu or just a drink. Hospitals have nice restrooms and some have doors that lock. The lock is good if you need privacy to wash up. Feminine supplies can be improvised out of toilet paper or paper towels.

The nicest free restrooms are in libraries or capitol buildings. Remember that the government is "we the people of the people for the people"!

Pets and homelessness companionship, emotional support comfort in your loneliness and protection from dangerous predators.

Earning money when you have no address or phone.

Getting along with people without using money.

Homelessness and mental illness a leading reason for being homeless. Drop out of society. Not able to stay in one place and get along with other people. Running scared and running away from problems. "Wherever you go there you are!"

Travelling at the poverty level. Walking, Hitch hiking, busses, Greyhound busses riding the Dawg.

Dumpster diving

"What's she doing?" I asked. "She's shopping." My friend replied as his wife looked in a dumpster in Billings, Montana. Anything in the trash is fair game. Help yourself. Look out for spoiled food garbage or filth like dirty cat litter. In Olympia there was a dumpster behind a grocery store dubbed by students to be the potato chip dumpster. For some reason it often contained perfectly good sealed bags of chips.

Once downtown in Olympia when I was pregnant I found figures of Jesus and Mary and Joseph. We figured it was from a disgruntled Catholic. We took the figures home and set them up on a window sill.

Rainbow Valley is a place South of Olympia that floods in the spring. I sang to Lee there once and we were surrounded by rainbows and in the company of puppy Moses while we were courting. In the summer it is a free campground for hippies, gypsies and musicians.

Free camping can be found all over Montana and Alaska. Just clean up after yourself. "Leave only footprints and take back only memories." according to John Muir.

Fee camping arrive late and leave early

Road trip from Seattle to Boston on $100 with Doug. We drove a car borrowed from A-1 Auto Movers for the cost of gas and a refundable deposit. We stayed in campgrounds and enjoyed fruit stands and Wendy's restaurant all you can eat salad bars. The trip was fun and affordable.

I remember seeing my grandmother's home where my father had grown up on a hill overlooking the great Mississippi river. I did not knock on the door because I didn't want her to meet Doug as I knew I would never marry him. He courted me for two years before I even kissed him. I'll always regret not knocking on the door and seeing her.

I only met her once and only for 1 day. She wrote to me about visiting and I didn't receive her letter as I was in Leavenworth. Grandma Gladys had thick waist length white hair. She was beautiful. We ate breakfast together before her flight out. She cried when she told me her husband Jick had passed away. I found my emotions confused and my eyes dry as I'd never met him. Grandma Gladys and I wrote letters throughout my childhood. She was very upset that I wanted to have a home birth. She died the day Seth was born. I called and spoke with Jon and his sisters Barbara and Ann on that day. I told them that I wanted to make a legal statement. I said that everything I wanted to inherit from her I had received during her lifetime. Jon said she was a millionaire at the time of her death. I'm not sure if he was exaggerating or telling the truth.

Train trip from Georgia to Washington. I was leaving my job and my boyfriend and going home, to Leavenworth, then anticipating college at The Evergreen State College in the fall. I got on the train with all my earthly belongings in 3 black steamer trunks and a back pack. They had cute little pillows they handed out. The rattle of the wheels lulled me to sleep. The train had a dining car which was expensive. A nice elderly lady treated me to breakfast since she wanted my company. The trip went North along the East coast then I changed trains in Chicago.

In Chicago I had a sinus headache and bought some Dristan. Then I groggily fell asleep on one of the hard benches in the station. I woke with 4 minutes to catch my train. I flashed a $20 bill at a bell cap and he loaded my trunks quickly onto the train as last call was announced. The train was named The Empire Builder. I found myself in the smoking car sitting next to a man with a cigar. He explained that I was in the smoking car so I moved.

The train seats were wide and reclined. Best of all they swiveled so that 4 seats would face each other and I could stretch out and sleep when the car wasn't crowded. We crossed hundreds of lakes in Minnesota. I remember the magnificent beauty of Glacier National park. There an arctic fox with pink fur ran near the train tracks. The fox has white fur in the winter and red fur in the summer. I saw him in the fall when his coat was changing. The dome car provided awesome views of mountains, lakes and rivers.

The rail yards often passed through industrial parts of cities. I saw rust, rubble and graffiti. My faithful grandparents met me at the train station in Wenatchee. We drove home to their house by the Wenatchee river in Leavenworth. Then I got a waitress job at Edel Haus. It was a bed and breakfast near the little hospital that was owned by a couple. The man brow beat his wife and was rude and loud towards me too.

I served my beloved friend Elizabeth and her mother breakfast. Elizabeth had returned from studying ceramics in Spain. When I was done with my shift I walked home. I saw Molly, Elizabeth's mother, and waved. She was in a daze and didn't respond. Finally she told me to go talk to Elizabeth who was waiting for me down by the river. I saw Elizabeth waiting on a rock. She explained how she had been feeling ill. I asked about it and she told me that she would be better in about 9 months. Eventually it occurred to me that she was unexpectedly pregnant. Her lover was in Spain. We sat together surrounded by the beauty of the river and made plans. I promised to help. She had never intended to marry or have children.

I briefly returned to Georgia. My boyfriend had called me in a drunken moment and promised to marry me. I made some arrangements including getting invitations printed. Once there, the dream of marriage fell apart and I burned the invitations on a bar B Q grill at a home where he was house sitting. The professor who owned the house came home. I was shamed beyond belief. Shortly thereafter I cut my losses and flew home to Leavenworth, pissed off.

I moved to Olympia. There I found a room in a house and a job. The first week college started my financial aid still wasn't finalized. So I sent some beautiful flowers to the financial aid office and signed the card with my social security number. Pell grants followed.

The first week of school my boyfriend showed up in his truck. I was glad that he brought our cat Joannabelle. I flipped out and got quite manic. He followed me to school and told the school councilor that I might be suicidal. So I got involuntarily committed to St. Peter's Hospital. There I remember throwing a book at my boyfriend and saying, "Peter Peter pumpkin eater had a wife and couldn't keep her." I felt that he put me in mental hospitals to control me. Once I was in, he would call all my relatives and get lots of attention.

Despite 5 hospitalizations that year I completed my course of study at The Evergreen State College in the program Health: Individual and Community. I was on a quest to discover health and my place in the community. My boyfriend and I lived in a basement apartment on Puget Sound. Our landlord was the dean of students. He did landscaping work and erosion control in exchange for rent. It is my theory that every time I tried to break up with him, he would get me committed. Once in he would visit me and refer to me as his fiancée' even though there never was a ring.

Elizabeth lived in Leavenworth with her mother. I sent her many books and quite a lot of chocolate during her pregnancy. When her baby boy was born we visited the next day. I remember her mother and father took a vacation together and I stayed with Elizabeth. She got all kinds of energy and painted the inside of the rental house white. I helped with baby Marlo and we celebrated.

At the end of the school year I was committed for the final time at St Peter hospital. This time 2 cops dragged me out of my bedroom window with the mental health professional watching. I resisted and bit the antenna off of the cop car. This time I was in for only a few days then released by the judge. I had come into contact with a student organization called SACRED. Student's Alliance For Constitutional Rights and Equal Determination under the law. They visited me in the hospital and offered outrage.

I met Lee Unterseher at Scotty's house. It was Paul who introduced us. I moved out of the Puget Sound home and into a white cottage on the edge of the forest near Evergreen. I left my boyfriend. He got some comfort from SACRED members at the Puppy Dog house. The Puppy Dog House was 5 men who lived together with a blonde Jennifer. She broke someone's microphone and I got blamed for it... yelled at then shoved against a cinderblock book case.

Lee scared me. But I found him strong and very smart. He was suing the Evergreen State College for forcing him to take psychiatric drugs then banning him from campus. SACRED members were involved in the lawsuit and in an underground newspaper called The Evergreen Free Press. A headline read, Student Sues Everyone Under The Sun.

I lived for a month at the white cottage with a house mate. There were trails through the woods to school. I remember one party with a bonfire and feasting. My friend Gaia the goat herd drummed and I danced.

Lee was in the military at Fort Lewis. He came down to visit me and we started dating. Pretty soon we were doing "it" "For God and Country." As Lee put it. Lee was the first man I had met who wanted to be a father. I fell deeply in love with him. He had a tape of Christian music called Fatherlove. That summer Lee's sister Diana had a baby girl and named her Jennifer. This we took to be a good sign. My cat Joannabelle really thrived at the white cottage and started hunting and leaving offerings on the front porch. She killed rabbits, snakes, birds and rodents. We nicknamed her Joanna Dianna The Huntress.

Free and low cost food resources on base. Better food at the air force base.

Alternative dwellings: teepee, yurt, cave, box car, car, tent, RV, under a bridge, cot in your cubicle, grain silo, barn, tent, cardboard box, semi-truck cab, house ape vs. house guest, house sitting, squatting. The pitfalls of RV's and mobile homes. Parks, lot rent congestion. clubhouses. Recurring nightmare of the mobile home park next to Interstate 5 by McCord Air Force Base.

Safe sources of potable water. Water filters, bleach, Iodine tablets

Getting out of the weather. Bus stations, train stations, shelters, libraries. Travelling at night and sleeping in rest areas during the day. The dangers of parks. Nevermind the bears, beware the human predators. Sometimes nature brings out the best in people. Avoid tearooms in parks on Capitol Hill Seattle. Frequenting National Parks. Arrive late and leave before dawn at campgrounds. Camp for free all over Montana. Seek out the wide open spaces.

The traveling man who loved his grandma. Staying clean, started on the road in the 1960's still on the go in the year 2002. The free cabbages, gleaning from the fields. Sleeping in the open fields, travelling to warmer climate zones human migration. Having a backpack and sleeping on it so no other transient could steal it. Hitch hiking and riding the railroads. Abandoned cabins, did shudder to think that I picked him up near the state penitentiary. Gave him $20 and said it was from my late father Jon Thomas Millhouse. He thanked me for being a, "Stand up girl."
Include all significant others religious transformations, churches and jobs.

Catholic, Mormon, Episcopalian, Lutheran, Pagan, Spiritualist,

Baha'i Faith.

Jamey, Sneaking around. My childhood home his childhood home.. The tree in Volunteer Park. Jimi Hendricks grave. Lion O Reilley and B.J. Monkeyshines restaurant on Broadway Newport Senior High School.
Doug (and Dan), Bellevue Community College and Shoreline Community College. The Four Season's Olympic Hotel. The garden Court then Room Service the voluntary ward at Harborview Hospital. Overlake Hospital in Bellevue.

Athens Georgia The Po Dunk family Mexican Place, The Snooty French Restaurant where I got fired. The Ramada Inn. There was a couple who sang in the lounge, "That's the POWER of love!" University of Georgia French and Spanish classes. The Stress Management Group.
Denny, Brasil's Early Learning Center. Radiance Herbs and Massage. St Peters Hospital
 Jordan in Atlanta,
Lee father of my firstborn son Seth Zared Emanuel Unterseher., Brian
safe stable creative genius who brings art, music and movies home and vowed to weather transient upheavals (and boy howdy there are some!) in our wedding vows.

Some bitching about how I worked 3 jobs at once. Summarize social security statement.

Jennifer J. T. Whitewing
1450 West Highland View Drive Apt. E - 104
Boise, Idaho   83702
Home Phone   343 - 5987
Cell Phone   869-8844

QUALIFICATIONS

Since 1985, I have been a Licensed Massage Therapist in the state of Washington.

Since 2003, I have been a Licensed Massage Therapist in the city of Boise.

Professional Member of the American Massage Therapy Association.

I have four years experience in home health care, two years experience as a Certified Nurse Assistant in a nursing home, eighteen years experience as a LMT.

I served in AmeriCorps National Service as a volunteer coordinator for Mid- Yellowstone Valley Habitat For Humanity.

WORK HISTORY

Massage Therapist, Simple Kneads Massage Therapy
I gave massage therapy and spa treatments in a day spa environment.

Volunteer Coordinator, Mid-Yellowstone Valley Habitat For Humanity
I recruited, trained and supervised volunteers for the construction of 3 homes. I kept records and assisted with office work.

Certified Nurse Assistant, Parkview Convalescent Care
I assisted patients with activities of daily living including, dressing,

transfers, feeding, bathing under the supervision of LPNs and RNs.

Personal Care Attendant, West Mont Home Management
I assisted clients with daily living activities, including bathing, physiotherapy, house cleaning, among many others, so that they could continue to remain in their homes.

Massage Therapist, Massage Therapy Associates
Under the supervision of a RN I performed massage therapy, scheduled appointments, collected fees, and filed forms at an office at the Holiday Inn.

Massage Therapist, Biofeedback and Stress Management Clinic
I performed filing, record keeping, assisting with exercise programs, massage therapy for chronic pain clients.

EDUCATION
Bachelor of Arts, The Evergreen State College, Olympia, WA 1989
Massage Therapy Certificate, Brenneke School of Massage, Seattle WA 1985
Connective Tissue Massage Certificate, Brenneke Institute, 1985
Certificate, The Institute Of Children's Literature, 1994
Workshops attended: First Aid, Polarity, Foot Reflexology, Hot Stone Massage,
Elder Massage, Myofascial Release, Trigger Point Therapy.

REFERENCES
Available upon request
Below is my earnings from my social security statement. I work hard and often 2 part time jobs or self employment. Yet see how little money I earn! ARGH!

My social security statement.   1980 $488
1981 $770
1982 $2,335

1983 $8,405
1984 $6,145
1985 $4,075
1986 $1,175
1987 $5,037
1988 $0
1989 $0
1990 $274
1991 $3,225
1992 $5,729
1993 $10,766
1994 $11,877
1995 $2,863
1996 $5,258
1997 $8,058
1998 $6,820
1999 $6,296
2000 $7,591
2001 $12,549
2002 $9,049
2003 $4,779

Chapter 27

AFTER THE CUSTODY BATTLE

My first husband and I had a stormy four year marriage followed by a divorce and custody battle nearly as long as the marriage. We have one son. The arrangement ended up as joint custody with Lee having primary physical custody and me having frequent visitation.

I did not want it this way. I do not like it. But what matters is that it works. Our son is doing fine.   His well being is more important than his parent's power struggles.

We separated when our son Seth was 3. During that time Seth lived with his father 4 days per week and me 3 days per week. This was based on my work schedule, not on parenting ability. Then Lee moved. I followed 150 miles away, settling in a strange city I didn't want to live in just to be near Seth.

We fought in the courts until we ran out of time and money. Then Lee moved again. Visitation was mediated in the courts and I remember driving 100 miles across the frozen wind swept praries of Montana to rendezvous with Lee and Seth every other weekend. It was a stressful and hazardous drive when the ice lay on the road in sheets and the blizzards blew. Seth adjusted well to all the travelling. He slept in the car or played games.

When school started for Seth he needed some stability. So he visited me on vacations. Lee moved with Seth three more times. I did not follow them as Lee told me the moves were temporary. Also there were no work opportunities for me in the remote towns.

When you create a child with someone it is a permanent bond. Memories of our lawyers have faded. They helped us to set up rules and they helped themselves to our money. The lawyers don't matter anymore.

All that remains is the best interests of the child Seth. We don't argue anymore. We discuss. We negotiate. We discuss Seth's activities and progress and we negotiate visitation. On major holidays Lee and I alternate having our only son.

Sometimes I am ashamed that I don't have custody of my son. Oftentimes I try to avoid telling acquaintances about my situation. Always I miss him. I call him several times a week and he calls back. I try to write him a letter or a post card every day. Seth saves the post cards. It is fun to send him new and educational ones. He rarely answers the letters. He says he is too busy. At least I get cards from Seth on major holidays like Mother's Day and my birthday.

Valentines' Day is bittersweet to me. It was the day the court appointed guardian ad litum decided that Seth would be better off with his father than with me. I presented her with positive information about myself and my family. Lee presented her with negative information about me. He got all his army buddies to write derogatory statements. She believed the evidence as it was presented to her. After all these years I have forgiven her. Still my life with my son moving away from me all the time has been very difficult.

When he visits it is a joyful homecoming. We have a celebration, a party. I indulge him. I take him to all the latest movies and amusement parks. I buy him fresh berries and whipped cream even when they are costly. The grocery bill jumps up 50%. I take time off from work to be with him. I am making up for lost time. The days of his childhood are fleeting and I love him so.

Seth is 11 now. He does very well in school and enjoys soccer, wrestling, piano, percussion and Boy Scouts when he is with Lee. Lee is a dedicated father who is involved is Seth's activities. When he visits me Seth relaxes, plays computer games, watches movies and is working on his first action adventure fantasy novel on the word processor.

"He is a blessing." Lee once said. On this we agree. In fact we find a lot to agree on these days. Pleasant, humorous e-mails are exchanged. I pay child support every month. Lee and I negotiate visitation with tact and diplomacy and always compromise in Seth's best interest.

Lee is good at providing structure for Seth. I am good at letting

Seth be spontaneous. Our co-parenting succeeds where our marriage failed. And we all benefit. Life is good!

Chapter 28

LOVE YOU INFINITY

I remember my gentle mother. Mother believed in me when I was struggling and unable to see hope in my own life. Mother was the one constant in a confusing string of changing addresses and changing relationships. For many years we lived a long way from each other but my mother encouraged me through the years as we kept in contact through letters, phone calls and e-mail. I saved every letter. We saw each other as often as possible given the distance between us. I always thought with certainty that my mother would live for a long time and that one day when she was a widowed great grandmother she would come to live with me. Instead I would come from Montana to Washington to be with her as she died of cancer.

My mother cared for infants and toddlers for her thirty year career. She was a loving mother and I was her only daughter, her only child. She advocated for children in South Africa and as a result she fostered a very special correspondence with Archbishop Desmond Tutu which blossomed into a deep friendship of letters.

On July 8th Peggy wrote to me: "My one,

Just another note to tell you, that I love you more than love. Your love will sustain me on surgery day. Love infinity, Mom"

Her sisters Lesley and Jean, parents Peg and Bill and I came together at her bedside and stayed in a wing of the hospital called Providence Inn to be close to her at any hour of the night and day.

What is the meaning of someone in their 50's going from healthy to dead in three months? This devastating cancer grew so fast. Those were three months filled with turmoil, loss, confusion and pain.

Diary entries: I left Montana in a hurry on the 28th after hearing that she had nearly died from the treatment.

7/30/99 I woke at 5:30 am and went downstairs to see my mother. She woke up with a gentle surprised smile.

"Oh hello." she murmured sleepily. She was glad to see me. I braided her hair and put an purple orchid in it. Her in laws had sent orchids from Hawaii. She found respite in moments of lucidity between cycles of pain. The pain medicine was on a drip plus she could push a button for more every ten minutes. The nurse Sue explained how the tumor had grown to the size of a grapefruit and she had fluid building up in her abdomen.

When her husband Jay visited in the evening, Peg, Bill and I went to dinner in the hospital cafeteria together to let Jay and Peggy have time alone. Afterwards I went to Jay's house and we talked heart to heart.

"I don't want to lose my mother."

"I don't want to lose my wife."

8/1/99 When I arrived in the morning Peggy had kicked off all her covers. The nurse helped her up in her chair. She ate a hearty breakfast. Then she napped. While she slept I drew crayon drawings of her immune system fighting and overcoming the cancer. When Dr. Goldberg came in to check on my mother he said that they were good clear drawings.

8/3/99 Lesley was up and Peggy was alert by the time I went downstairs. Jean came with her son Douglas. Brother Willy came in the early evening. We got Peggy up in the wheeled lounge chair three times. The first time we took her to a sunny nook where she ate some lunch. Then we wheeled her to the chapel which was quite an undertaking because of the big, heavy, reclining chair and the large IV stand with three IV's going into her shoulder. We sang hymns in the chapel. The third time up we stayed in the room and didn't wheel her anywhere.

8/5/99 Peggy was up early. Peg and Bill came down in mid-morning. Jean arrived, Willy came around noon. Jay visited. Peggy was full of joy to see him. She spoke of her fear of dying and how it felt to be so ill. Her pain was intense.

I kept calling her Mommy Love. She said, "It isn't easy being your mother." It touched a sensitive place in my heart. I remembered dark times I depended on her to guide me, and times I had been hostile and angry. She always forgave me. Now was the time to give back. Now I was the adult. When she was confused and disoriented I tried to gently guide her around.   She sensed my impatience so I had to pray for grace or I would upset her dignity.

8/23/99 Monday Jean visited. We took Peggy up to the fifth floor room with the view of Mt. Rainier. I'm not sure whether or not she saw it. She seemed to look at me. Jean went back for Peggy's glasses, still she looked at me. Then we went to the chapel and sang How Great Thou Art.   Peggy sang along. My mother silently put my hand on the statue of Jesus. She ate a little dinner then woke for Jay's visit to say, "I love you."

He said, "I love you infinity."

Peggy had been started on hospice care. The treatment had failed. The cancer grew. When asked by the doctor if she wanted to be revived when she died she said, "No." When asked how she felt about death she said, "It will be a great adventure."

9/1/99 to 9/4/99 Long vigil at Peggy's bedside. A very efficient and up beat hospice nurse named Dixie checked in on her daily. Peggy stopped eating and I really missed feeding her. I tried feeding her and Lesley stopped me saying that I wasn't doing it for her but for myself. I started eating her hospital meals so I could stay in the room with her. It felt as if I was being nourished by my mother.

9/5/99 In the morning Peg called me downstairs to Peggy's room as the nurse Sue had a difficult time finding Peggy's blood pressure. I rested under white cotton blankets in the lounge chair all day listening to my mother breathe. I told her that I would be OK, my aunts and uncle, Lesley, Jean, and Willy would be there for me. I tried to hold my voice steady as I said this. It was difficult. I had to draw strength from God.

My mother died at 7:20 p.m.. amidst songs, my flute playing and laughter. I started playing Silent Night and I was so nervous that I couldn't get the key right so I tried three different keys. The room filled with laughter as they tried to sing along. Bill and Peg, Lesley and I were with her all day. Near the end Sister Claire the nun, Molly the CNA, and Ron the RN joined us. We sang Ode to Joy. Bill sobbed. Sister Claire said that the song would, "Open the gates of heaven." Peg and Lesley sang Peggy's special lullaby from childhood. After she died Ron listened to her chest and confirmed that her heartbeat had stopped. I covered her up with the bright, silky, yellow wrap that Lesley brought from Greece. At my request Lesley removed mother's wedding ring and gave it to me. It fit on my little finger.

I called Jay and he said he was glad that it was I who let him know.

On Monday Archbishop Desmond Tutu called and prayed with Jay over the phone, he later sent flowers.

I struggled for answers to the questions that many who have lost a loved one to cancer ask. What was the purpose? Why did she have to suffer like that? What possible higher good could be found? The answer was love. A great deal of love surrounded my mother. The whole family drew closer to one another. The graceful nurses tended to her with compassion and kindness. God is love. My mother's illness and death brought us closer to the real meaning of life which is to love one another. I remember she often said, "I love you infinity". I'm certain that her love does go on.

It goes on when I teach my son about things his grandma used to say. I feel her love in old letters and verses that she wrote. I remember her with pictures and every time I light a candle. My aunts, uncle and grandparents lend their support and share memories. Her love blazes forth in a quilt she embroidered for Seth. My Godmother sends old photos and tells stories. Although my beloved mother is no longer here on earth, I still feel her love because I love her infinity.

INTRODUCTION

Mommy
I love you. How could you go so soon and so far away? Do you see me holding Nanny's arm? Do you see me longing for Seth, loving Brian, writing Jean and Lesley, calling Jay?
I hope you see me. I know you love me infinity. You have gone beyond me into the ethereal realm where there is time enough for love.

MOTHER LOVE LOST

Time. I always thought my mother would live longer and there would be more time. Time for discovering each other, time to figure out our differences, time for being together for my mommy to play with my son, her only grandchild.

Last night I cried out in agony that my love for my mother had not been enough, that I had caused her heartache and pain. And her spirit came to me on the breeze and rubbed my back and sang my goodnight song from childhood.

The wind sings soft in the mountain breeze, the lake shore sounds so gaily, it's Jennifer's song in the mountain air, all for my little baby. And all for the wind that sings so soft and all for the water sparkles, It's Jennifer's song in the mountain air, all for my little Baby.

By Pegasus   November 3,1978

"...We know we are not alone..."
Dr. Martin Luther King Jr.

Trinity Unthroned
"You don't love him,"
Said the shrink, "you didn't know him long enough."
"You don't love him."
Said the mother, "you only felt sorry for him."
"You don't love him,"
Said the father, "you were only attracted."
I believed for 14 years
But in the endless time space of our short and infinite time
together
I have all I need to
Disbelieve.

Jennifer Jaye

What did we create
That not-dark night
In the Alaskan summer?
Were we but the vessels
of a
Destiny?

Feather In Space
Blown to another space
Never again afraid
Grown to courage
To reach for the infinite
Cracking open
What once was sealed

"Was blind But Now I See"

In the stretching
The opening of
courage

Vistas of the stars unfold
Where suns are rising
On a new
Universe

The Source
Winging my way into the
Sun of a far-reaching
Sea
I feel the chill
And thrill
Of your
infinity

Mount To Ra

Three- .
"The soul selects her own society
then bars the door
On her divine majority
obtrude no more."
Emily Dickinson

That only three
Could call the eagle in me
To the sun

One has gone to the
Realm of spirit
One I live and love with every
day
And one challenges
The center of my reality

With an earthquake
That shakes the
stars

Caring
A new-born bird
A galaxy's reach
Speak the vastness of
Me

In the spaces you climb
Where your intellect soars
Another infinity

Is it too late to bring that
Tiny bird song
To your
Eternity?

Gifts
You gave me a daughter
From an almost-nothing life-germ
To an almost-woman
Wrapped in rain-struck sun

You came again

To water me with tears
So that when a sun shines
I'm in a rainbow

Candle Flame
Passing to the other side of
Forty
Remember
I love you

Eternity In Our Moment
Come to me again
To the song of our
Budding daughter

To the tears and light
of my new love for you

Remember that first day by the fire
When we smiled over her?

Offspring

I study her beauty
And think of you.
Life-explosion
Incredible reverence
For all that's lovely:
Our Jennifer

Bonding

So many love her
yet
You and I
Feel our futures
Turning
In that infinitely graceful
Life

Gone Love

Did we both only
Want
Or did we give to a state of
Wanting
Because we wanted so much to give?
Wanting
To desperation
To fear, then anger
To hatred

Years later
Chasms bridged

Joined

A rope of pain
Held us together
For many years

Until faint
Starlight
Set it
Gleaming

Shining Fair One
The crystals
Her dark hair

A star
In the Night
of
us

To Jon
Thank you for the
Cool water
From my reservoir

You gave it to me today
As I lay weary
On a Friday morning break

As I drank from your hands
I kissed them

Ra's Legacy
To aspire to give
when before, we only drained

Jennifer
Beautiful, self-lost
struggling, growing, crying
Like a trapped Eagle
Mine

Jon
Tormented, splendid
Thinking, hurting, loving
Like a lonely Eagle
Gone

The Colors of Growth
Fifteen years of
Awakening to
Brahman

Her flowering
Towering
Showering
Rainbow.

Before The Fall
Cutting edge of suffering
like a dark and somber sky
Struck once with Light.

North Into Spring
Yesterday
I climbed up off

the last step of
Despair
Into a place where
Sun shines
and Flowers bloom

Eagle and Dove
You in your waste of
Construction camp
Where womanless men
Curse and fight,

You come from fourteen hours in snow
On color drained Tundra
Back to an empty bed
Wracked with dark awakenings

My solitude keeps a shrine
Where my love worships your need
Where your homeless heart
Will always have a Home

Shield Of Brightness
When Jennifer first shone in my arms
Tears burst forth
Because she looked like you
Tears of love
Tears of light
Tears of Joy
Instinct bared my breast to her
Illumination of our love
In that exquisite bundle
But doctor power boomed
Neurosis!

Slapped me with librium's fog
Deadening love, light, joy....

As the world has tried to darken you and I
These twenty years:
"Your fundamental light is wrong.
It is wrong to be who you are."

Facing this mercury vapor blast
I've earned a raw reckless courage
I serve the rainbow and myself.

My light-spirit and Jennifer's shining Force
Stream through twenty year gone tears
Like the Iridescence of the Love
We're learning to share

Hello! Gruenzi! Brigates!
I'm O.K. and It's kind of tough,
but I believe things will be better now.
There is still much work to do.
Love, Jon

One Came From High
She climbed to enchantment
Through dark valleys
And steep rocks

She saw larch
Light
Lake Leprechaun,
Lake Vivianne

She came again

To our home enclosure
I never knew all I had worried
In her years of searching
Until I saw the sun
In her larch tree eyes.

Father and Daughter
Jennifer's picture shines
Nineteen at Enchantment Lakes
Soul-found

Your card arrived last night.

For the first time in eternity
I Believed your soul
Could ever be
Found

Birth of my Divine
That dark Good Friday
My foundations
Crashed in terror

As our baby slept
I feared for her life,

My emotions
Shook with earth,

Our marriage rocked
Out of control,

And dreams broke into
A thousand splinters,

But Sunday
Easter came.

I Will Lift Up Mine Eyes
I've woven a rope of
Love, Light, Hope, Poetry, Strength, Infinity

We're roped together
On the hardest climb of my life

Cliffs hover over
Crevasses so deep
They reach to Hell

The way is dangerous
Exhausting
Complex
We're climbing to a high summit
To behold
Brocken's bright spectre

I know a guide:
"I believe that unarmed truth and unconditional love
  will have the final word in reality."
"... We are not alone..."
"...I have been to the mountaintop..."
Dr. Martin Luther King Jr.

Dr King taught me to think
Not of the abrasions on my back (and heart)
But of what would happen
to you
If you fell.

No miles apart, no shock
To our rainbow rope
can ever
sever
My caring.

Vision
We five stepped
From a log cabin
Into a radiant meadow
We danced together
As we never have
In society's world

We came to a crystal mountain
lake
Jon dipped deep
Gave water to our children
Growing now so tall
He held full hands to my lips
And I drank till my soul was
shining
I offered water to Jon
But instead he gave me more
of his

Then we five danced away
Into the tinges of orange
Indian Paintbrush.

Dandelion

He comes in peace...

Sometimes in the web
Of my approaching sleep
Fear's faces advance
Faces of evil,
More potent fear
Of invoking that dark
Myself.
Always I hear
"You are not alone."
Dr. Martin Luther King Jr.
Speaks to my solitude
And I am
Invincible.

Man of love on the other side
You penetrate the impenetrable,
A sun shaft on a stream
A gleam of sun on a
  dandelion

In a child's hand.

C'est Finis

Chapter 29

Memoir of My Mother
Summer Of 1999

I wrote an e-mail on June 25th, 1999: Dear Grandma Jini and Grandpa Jim,

Brian, Seth and I had a wonderful time at the family reunion and quality time with Jay and Peggy on either end of the 10 day vacation.

We toured Seattle and saw lots of art and nature movies at the IMAX dome theater and the Pacific Science Center's 3-D theater. The 3-D theater was showing Into The Deep, a show about the ocean. People were reaching out to touch the fish!

We had a mellow time at the ocean. Many Starks were there and several of Peg's nieces. There were 40 people coming and going all week and it was lovely to have quality time with everyone. We went to the ocean daily. It was too cold to swim in but Seth waded in the surf. The weather was really sunny and nice and that was a real blessing since we were in the rain forest.

Clearwater House, the house we rented, was spacious enough to sleep 20 at a time. It had a lovely yard with rhododendrons, roses and cala lilies blooming. There was a pond with singing frogs and a little path to the river nearby.

Everyone except Peggy was very well. Peggy, my mother has this persistent pain so that she can't sit down. She did not come to the reunion but we saw her for 4 days anyway. When we returned to the house we drove by to go to the waterfall. But Peggy sensed us and came out so we stopped. She had provided a gourmet snack tray with roma tomatoes, olives and beef.

Peg and Bill were sleeping extra and gaining weight. Willy was very happy with Wendy. His sons Will and Rory climbed Mt. Rainier with Rory's friend Stacia.

Jean's son Leroy is working construction laying foundations. Douglas is attending high school. Both brothers are very involved with search and rescue.

Lesley was in excellent health and gave everyone Reike sessions. It is a form of energy healing. Mike is working in silicon valley with internet gaming. He is married to a lovely Japanese born wife Kaoru. Whitney is married with a two year old son Merce, a wife Monica and a stepson Ryan. Whitney is a college professor in upstate New York. Whitney's family missed the reunion because they were moving into a new house.

Peg is one of the last surviving members of her family of 8 so her nieces and nephews come a long ways to see her.

Bill's sister in law Marian came from Vermont with 6 family members: John Sherwood, Ben, Karen, Jeff and Carma. Fortunately Carma's daughter Audrey was 12 and played well with Seth. We all feel strengthened and blessed.

Sylvia called Jay on Father's Day! I'm sure he e-mailed you all about it. It brought great joy to all of us. Brenna sounded great too. They are living in Bozeman, Montana. What a special place. Well God bless you. Love to all. Peace be with you. Love Jennifer

Peggy wrote on May 27: Beloved Jen,

Thanks for your letter and also your card, which came today. I was so sorry to hear of Dan's mother, send he and Rachael my love.

Turns out the lab tests say no bladder infection, and I'm going to see my doctor Saturday to rule out other possibilities. Knowing that I don't have a bladder infection is encouraging. If I feel good enough by Saturday, they said I could cancel the appointment. I may go just to be sure, I want to be in top health for my morning job. It's funny - coming back to this job I seem to have put back on the cloak of confidence I left behind there. It feels right. I get a sense of peace often after I make a decision, and I had that when I hired back on. I get a lot of peace as I work there too.

The new director seems promising. She is very smiley and gets a lot done. So if my lagging health would get in gear, I have a good life. I think I'll be well soon; this is mostly stress related and the stress in my life is getting more manageable. Know my prayers are always with you. I love you infinity. Mum

Peggy wrote on May 29th: Jennifer Love,

Today I got a clean bill of health at the doctor's. All infections are cleared up. There will be some healing process. I can't say how much your cards, e-mail and caring meant. I am so blessed to have a daughter like you. Thanks for your short sleepy e-mail from Friday night. Love infinity, Pegasus Mum

Peggy wrote on June 26th: Dearest Daughter,

I loved your beautiful gracious thank you. That was a really heavenly time for us too. Jay really liked Brian and thought Seth was smart and charming. It would be wonderful if you took July off to be with Seth. It's wise of you to think of keeping occupied. But what a wonderful time together. How generous of Brian to suggest it.

Today my doctor was on vacation, and I saw a very level headed man doctor at the clinic. He found swelling and tenderness in my uterus. He said they need to do a biopsy July 9th to find out what is going on with my uterus. I will have an ultra sound July 16th, so by then they should have things checked out. My fibroids are growing. This doctor will work with my regular doctor. He also treated me for a possible bladder infection which will be cultured by the time I see my doctor Tuesday.

I'm starting to wonder about a hysterectomy. Please don't mention this to Nanny; it is speculation at this point. On the bright side, Jay went out last night to get me some cotton sheets, because I seem allergic to synthetics. Well, he came home with the most beautiful, comforting sheets and cotton comforter I've ever seen. Ecru lace on the sheets, and a fabulous quilt pattern with pillow covers. Every time I rest in these sheets I feel totally loved by Jay and by God. Love in all eternity, Pegasus Mum

Peggy wrote on July 2nd: Jen, I just can't tell you how much your beautiful card meant. I cherish it on the Dansk shelf. Knowing how much you care is all I need.

September 12th, when he comes back from vacation, I plan to switch to Dr. David McFarland. He seems very thorough and I like his way of presenting himself. The other doctor didn't seem to impact getting me well. Dr. McFarland immediately went to the uterus and abdomen where there were variations. Love, Mum

On July 8th Peggy wrote: My one,

Just another note to tell you, that I love you more than love. Your love will sustain me on surgery day. Love infinity, Mom

Nick Johnson wrote on July 18th: Jennifer

We visited with your mother yesterday. Both her and Jay are doing as well as can be expected. She is, of course, worried more about you and Jay than she is about herself, but that is to be expected given her nature. If she can keep some of that strong faith she has developed the last few years, and feel positive about her life, she should be able to continue keeping a better spin on life as it is. Yesterday was most likely her worst day (based on my experience with surgery), as the real "sleeper" pain killers are now gone and she is facing both the pain and the reality of things. As she goes through these next few days, I think her ability to find the good in the world, and her inner strengths, will allow her to begin to feel a bit better about things, no matter what her decisions on the future direction of treatment may be. She is a beautiful person, and is suffering with all this in a way that still recognizes the good out there. She told Laurel and I how great we looked, and talked about the wonderful music the hospital plays in the morning, rather than dwelling on that which no one is able to control at this time. Jay is, I think, full of turmoil on the inside, but is working hard to keep up a front so Peggy will find him strong while she needs him to be. They are a very devoted couple, and this is drawing them into each other deeper than most of us ever are able. Keep up the words of support for her, and whatever she wants to do, let her have her head and go for it. I know she cares for you more than anything in this world, and always remember that, for it is a strength you can rely on always. If you need anything or if we can help with something you think needs done, let us know. We will try to do what we can. And I'll keep checking on both Peggy and Jason and try to offer up good vibes and hope as best I can. Love to you, Nick

I wrote to my cousin Whitney on July 20th: Dear Whitney,

My mother, Peggy, starts treatment with Interleukin-2 today at the hospital. She has melanoma in her lower abdomen and the doctor recommended treatment with interleukin-2. It is a natural substance that will stimulate her immune system. The treatment will last for 2 weeks.

When I talked to her yesterday she sounded very shaky. She is terrified of dying. She was in a lot of pain and had an acid stomach ache. I told her to take advantage of the hospital pain relievers and to ask for an antacid. Thank you for writing to her. I'm sure she enjoyed getting a letter or card from you. I am very concerned about my mother. At the same time I'm trying to have a joyful summer with Seth. He'll be with me for one more week then he will be with his father. They have one week vacation then sports start. Seth is very active in sports. Take care. Enjoy your little family. I love you. Love Jennifer

On July 22nd Jay wrote: Dear Jen,

Nannie mentioned, that you were considering coming to Seattle to visit your Mother after Seth's visit was over. Peggy wants to have a "Honey Moon" with me, the first week out of the hospital. I was thinking it would be good for your Mom and you to spend the second week with us and take care of her while, I am at work. Let Jean do the third week. If that will not work out for you. I think you are the only other person in the world, that your Mom would agree to for her "first week" care giver. Love Jason

On July 23rd I wrote: Dear Grandpa Jim and Grandma Jini,

I heard about the lovely flowers that you sent my mother and I wanted to thank you personally. It always helps to have a room filled with flowers.

Seth, Brian and I are fine. Seth returns to Lee next Monday. After that I may go to Washington to help out my mother when she gets home from the hospital.

I hope and pray that you are well. I'm very interested in shark cartilage. How do you get some? It can do no harm and maybe it will do some good. Jay sounded strong on the phone last night. Peggy is really sleeping and resting a lot so he suggested that I cannot call but that she would call out.

In Alta Vista I keyed in: melanoma, interleukin-2, clinical trials and found thousands of sites. It sounds like a very promising treatment.

Take care. I love you. Thanks again for the rare and lovely flowers that you sent Peggy. Love Jennifer

On July 24th Jim White wrote: Dear Jennie,

We were, of course, very happy to share some of our tropical flowers with Peggy and do hope that she does enjoy 'em. The orchids last so well that they are nice in a bouquet.

We, too are horrified about Peggy's illness and pray for her all the time. Our church group and the Pahoa Catholic church is also praying for her. Guess, that is all we can do from here.

Glad you had a good summer with Seth. That was very nice and I guess it would be good if you could go and help your mom when she does get home from the hospital. Take good care for we love you much and May God bless you all, Jim and Jini

On July 28th I wrote to Dan Geiger: Dear Dan,

Could you please pray for my mother Margaret Stark White at the holy shrines. She is very ill with Melanoma, a large cancer that is growing in her lower abdomen.

Seth returned to his father today. We had a great day with Brian staying home from work and a trip to South Park pool. Seth even had a free lunch in the park.

Summertime has been very sweet with Seth here. Thank you for your e-mail. I will be deeply grateful for any prayers that you could say for my beloved Mother. Sincerely, Jennifer Telander Whitewing

Dear Jennifer,

Be assured that your mother is in our prayers. May the healing she needs take place. I am sorry she has to go through this.

I am happy to hear you had an enjoyable summer centered around Seth and Brian. These will be times all of you will remember especially Seth. It does so much toward building the core and character of a young person.

With warm greetings from Carmel, Dan

On July 28th Whitney wrote: Jenny

I just got your brave letter. I am ringing and thronging in this news of how your mother is suffering. This Saturday as well, my family will be at my mother's house for a spiritual gathering, which I view as a chance to connect. What you plan sounds immensely caring. I will feel a parallel course. Much love, Whit

Brother Mike wrote on the same day: I wish I had seen her more recently. I haven't seen her in many years. I have wondered in recent years how many more times I would get to see grandmommy and granddad before the years took them away. but Peggy...this caught me by surprise that I haven't emotionally 'got' it yet.

On July 28th From lifetime friend Nick Johnson: Jennifer- I've talked a bit with Jason, most lately last night. He is holding up O.K., all things considered, but is obviously very concerned. We discussed maybe going over this weekend if Peggy is between treatments and responding, otherwise we won't. He talks some on the phone, which helps him get some of the emotion out, but I haven't yet convinced him to come by for a visit or dinner. Will try to keep an eye out for him. This is the time we all need to be strong and positive, and I think he is doing good on that front. Hang in there kiddo, and our love to you all. Nick

I responded: Dear Nick and Laurel,

Peggy's treatment with Interleukin-2 is having serious side effects. She is unable to speak and is asleep most of the time. Now is not a good time to visit. Calling is no good either. I call Jay at home in the evenings to cheer him up. There is some speculation about me visiting August 4th for a week. The doctor suggested that she would be recovered from the treatment and able to visit and maybe be home from the hospital. I'll call you when I do come out. Thank you for when you did visit and for the e-mail about the visit. Take care and have a great summer. Seth was with us in July and I took the whole month off from work to be with him. We went to the movies, an amusement park, several day hikes and he got to play a lot of computer games. It was really a sweet time. I hope you are all in good health and enjoying the sweet savors of summertime. Love Jennifer

Peggy's sister Lesley wrote on July 30th: Beloved, beloved Jenny,

Thank you for your beautiful letter. It expresses so much of what I also feel. Coming to terms with the incredible unfairness of life is hard, hard, hard! At the same time, my love for Peggy has blazed white hot, and I am feeling a powerful appreciation of the depth and wonder of her life, the connections she's made, her commitment to finding a path of light through a hell of a lot of darkness that life gave her.

But at times I'm also screaming at God for what's happening to her and just crying for my little sister.

You've probably been told I'm going to see her briefly, flying out Monday night and leaving on the red-eye Tuesday night, the day before you get there.

I love you very very much, and pray for you as Peggy said she wanted for herself, that this be a time of spiritual growth, which to me includes all the rage, pain, numbness, times of spiritual clarity and intense giving, rolling over in waves of grief's many faces and coming eventually to some sort of shore.

I am going to see Peggy now and keep the commitment I made to myself 8 years ago to myself of Tom's and my trip to Europe, which is from August 6 through 28. We will be in Romania, hopefully to see the total eclipse of the sun, and to visit and take pictures of the town which is the birth place of the adopted child of a friend and co-worker, a beautiful 9 year old child living with AIDS which he had at birth. They are excited about our bringing the pictures to him. Then we'll be in Greece, which is a spiritual journey I have always wanted to make. If Peggy dies while we're there, I'll come be with the family afterward. Dearest one, for whatever love can do, mine is with you. Love Lesley

On July 30th Miller Batson M.D. wrote: Dear Jen,

Thank you for keeping me updated on Peggy's condition. It has been hard watching her go through this. It must be really frustrating on her not being able to communicate back. Bill summed it up when he said, "I just feel so helpless."

I hope she clears up quickly and that your visit goes well. Also that she can get out of the hospital quickly, not that it is a bad place. Quite the contrary, I was impressed. Peg and Bill are just a few hundred feet from Peggy's room, the cafeteria food was good, with a good salad bar. There were plenty of decorations, photos, fish tanks, quiet spots and nice people.

So please keep me posted. I hope to pop in again over there

when I can. Love Miller

Chapter 30

My beloved mother Margaret "Peggy" Stark White died last September from melanoma cancer. She went home to be with the Lord who she loved with all her heart and soul. I had the honor of sharing her last pain filled months on earth with her and other family members. Her sisters Lesley and Jean, Parents Peg and Bill and I came together at her bedside and stayed in a wing of the hospital to be close to her at all hours of the night and day. Providence hospital had old parts built in the early 1900's maybe 1908. Then there was an added on part which was modern. In the oncology ward there were open visiting hours. Anytime was O.K. In the ward there were many rooms for private chats or to view outside. Bill liked to be in those rooms working on his Treatise On Beauty. Peg had her thyroid surgery in the old hospital many years ago. It was tricky to find our way around the hospital. It covered several city blocks. The hospital was situated on top of a hill in Seattle. There was a wonderful cafeteria downstairs with a salad bar, sushi, sandwiches and a grill. There was a refrigerator kitchen and laundry for the Providence Inn.

An e-mail to Archbishop Desmont Tutu on August 24th:

Jay & Peggy White wrote: Dearest Friend,

Peggy's surgery revealed an advanced, inoperable Melanoma Cancer. After the surgery she chose Interleuken2 "IL2" as the potentially most effective, but most dangerous treatment available. Prior to the beginning of the treatments, she said to tell Desmond that "we are going for the gold" if it (IL2) doesn't cure me, then "God has other plans for me." She nearly died twice during the first set of treatments of a course of four treatment sets. She has told me, "No more." She does not want to die in a comatose state connected to machines. She is currently resting peacefully with a close family member near her side nearly 24 hours a day in room 345 East at Providence Medical Center in Seattle. She said, "Send him my love and thank him for his friendship and support. Sincerely Jay and Peggy White

Dearest Friends,

Thank you for the heavy news. I have said some of these things to Peggy before. I am nothing if not repetitive.

St. Teresa of Avila once remonstrated with God because of a bout of suffering that she was experiencing, 'No wonder your friends are so few, considering how you treat them.' The friends of Jesus, His mother was found close to the Cross and it had been predicted that a sword would pierce her heart. The privilege of being God's friend is frequently a painful and demanding one. You are God's friend and so you will be found close to the cross. I have also said that we are sometimes asked to be Simons of Cyrene. He was forced to carry Our Lord's cross. God invites us to bear the cross with Christ for the salvation of the world. St. Paul frequently begged God to take away what he called a thorn in the flesh, but the Lord refused and said, "My grace is sufficient; my strength is made perfect in weakness. When you are weak then you are strong!" Paul spoke about a mystery in which we make up what is lacking in the sufferings of Christ.

You are God's child and so you should remonstrate with God as Job the Lord's servant did. Cry and rail at God. God is after all our father and mother. And this God is Immanuel who is there in the fiery furnace, there in the light and in the darkness, there in joy and in sorrow, there in life and death. Nothing can separate us from the love of God in this Jesus Christ. If you can, offer the pain, the frustration the anger, offer it up to God to use it for the benefit of the world. God actually has confidence in you, that you can do that whereas others would just rail against him and it would end there.

I love you and pray for you. Much love and God's blessings, Desmond.

Diary entries. 7/29/99 I left Montana in a hurry on the 28th. I planned a special healing service with Rosalie Marson for my mother. She said it would be a "Crossover ceremony." For the ceremony I was to go down to the Yellowstone river. Since I went to Seattle instead, I contemplated all the rivers I had to cross to get there. In Seattle I took a cab from the Greyhound bus terminal to the hospital. I went in the ER entrance since it was so late at night. Security called Peg and Bill in room 510 of the Providence Inn so that they could let me in. Providence Inn was a wing of the hospital for family of patients to stay close to their loved ones. There were two single beds Peg and Bill snuggled in one and I slept in the other.

7/30/99 I woke at 5:30 am and went downstairs to see Peggy. She woke up with a gentle surprised smile. I braided her hair and put an purple orchid in it. Her in laws had sent orchids from Hawaii. Peggy had moments of lucidity and cycles of pain. The morphine was on a drip plus she could push a button for more every 10 minutes. Her abdomen was swollen. The nurse Sue explained how the tumor was the size of a grapefruit and she had fluid building up in her abdomen. Peggy liked coffee and cereal, later soup and apple juice. She did not want to be left alone. Sister Jean called several times. I called the Johnsons and another friend Jimmy Hill. He said that he might visit. It was a long intense day. I followed Rosalie's instructions for the crossover ceremony. Later I placed the sacred stones in Peggy's little bonsai juniper tree.

Peggy didn't like the wrist restraints and fought them. They put them on to prevent her from pulling out her IV lines again. She had done this several times. The nasal canula for oxygen was irritating to her nose.

Sister in law Judy called. Husband Jay visited in the evening. Peg, Bill and I went to dinner together to let Jay and Peggy have time alone. I went to Jay's house and we had long heart to heart talks. "I don't want to lose my mother." "I don't want to lose my wife."

7/31/99 Sister in law Judy visited from Hawaii. We rode into Seattle with her friend Garth. Jean, Nephew Leroy, Peg, Bill, Judy and I took turns visiting so there was not more than 2 or 3 in the room at a time. Leroy hugged me in a huge bear hug. It was wonderful and strength giving. In the evening Peggy got up in her chair and wanted to go home. Jean took me aside and gave me some money that Marian Stark had sent. It helped me to stay and afford meals and bus tickets. Peggy tried for her IV lines again so they restrained her arms again. She detested the restraint.

8/1/99 When I arrived in the morning Peggy had kicked off all her covers. The nurse got her up in her chair. She was active all morning then napped. While she slept I drew crayon drawings of her immune system fighting and overcoming the cancer. Dr. Goldberg said that they were good. The nurse gave her medication to ready her for a cat scan. I went with her for the cat scan. She slept through the whole thing. A doctor had x-rayed flowers as art in the waiting room. They were delicate and beautiful.

8/2/99 Sister Lesley arrived after 10pm and slept at Peggy's bedside. There was a big soft chair that folded out into a narrow bed. Peggy was restless and anxious. Lesley said that she was honored to help Peggy with her process. She did some reike sessions on her in the night.

8/3/99 Lesley was up and Peggy was alert by the time I went downstairs. Douglas and Jean came. Brother Willy came in the early evening. We got Peggy up in the wheeled lounge chair three times. The first time we took her to a sunny nook where she ate some lunch. Then we wheeled her to the chapel which was quite an undertaking because of the big heavy chair and the large IV stand with three IV's going into her shoulder. We sang hymns in the chapel. Peggy said that the hospital had Starkitis and that it was wonderful. The third time up we stayed in the room and didn't wheel her anywhere. Peggy had egg for breakfast, soup for lunch and jello for dinner. Judy visited Whitney called. Lifetime friend Joni called 2 times. She wanted me to find a hotel that would allow her to bring her dog. I searched for almost an hour calling hotels and motels from the yellow pages. Then I gave Willy the chore. He eventually found one.

8/5/99 Peggy was up early and her wrists were restrained. As soon as I arrived they took her out of them. Peg and Bill came down in mid-morning.

Peggy fed herself breakfast while sitting up in a chair. She got dressed after breakfast. Peg brought a bright pink muumuu with flowers embroidered on it for Peggy to wear. Jean bought a banana rum sheet cake for the staff to thank them for caring for Peggy. I saved a piece for Mona a very special, strong, red haired CNA. Jean arrived, Willy came around noon. Jay visited. Peggy was full of joy to see him. She spoke of her fear of dying and how it felt to be so ill. Her pain was intense.

Leroy and his girlfriend Amanda came late. Leroy, Amanda, Peg and Bill visited with Peggy together. Peggy got her catheter out and her IV lines detached. She started on oral morphine for pain.

Ruth Evans came with barley green, papaya and carrot juice and shark cartilage. She went into Peggy who welcomed her joyously and told her that, "No matter what." her time in the hospital had been an enriching time. Later Ruth told me that she was very impressed at how I tactfully protected Peggy from too many visitors or too long visits. She brought nude baby pictures of Seth playing with water which were delightful.

8/6/99 Peggy was up early. She was very assertive, very grumpy. Peg Bill and I watched her. In the afternoon Bill checked into the ER to get some attention for his lungs. He had an oxygen reading of 95% which was excellent. To quote Dr. Seuss Bill is, "In pretty good shape for the shape that he's in."

Judy came in the afternoon. Peggy took many walks to the bathroom and to the fish tank in the corner room. One particular purple fish came up and made eye contact with us. I named him the Empathy Fish. She got disoriented about which room was hers. Jay visited for several hours. Dr. Goldberg talked of releasing her to the transitional care unit then home. Jay had concerns about her coming home.

8/7/99 Peggy was hypersensitive and irritable today. She was still on IV antibiotics. The nurse said she was up every half hour to the bathroom. She needed better quality sleep. She was unfocussed and disoriented and unable or unwilling to follow directions. Nick and Laurel Johnson visited. Jay visited too. At 8pm she pulled her IV out and it had to be tended to quickly by 2 nurses. I was so upset that I had to leave the room. I felt that she had endangered herself. She said that she wanted to live and expressed fear that she would never make love again. She ate frequently in small quantities. The nurse came into the room and thought Peggy's mother Peg was the patient.

8/8/99 I talked to Jay on the phone about Peggy coming home and how he's doing etc. he sounded good. Peggy was coherent, peaceful and sleepy. She nibbled on her food. She said, "I love you." and "How fun." when I told her that I was going to Port Townsend for a few days. Peg and Bill took an early lunch and nap.

8/9/99-8/10/99 I was resting in Port Townsend. On 8/10 I was up early with a phone call from Peg at 7:45 am. She said that Peggy was confused and didn't recognize her. I returned to the hospital in Seattle.

8/11/99-8/14/99 On 8/11 Peg and Bill went to Leavenworth. I stayed with Peggy at Providence Medical Center. We listened to Fairy Ring a dreamy tape and some country Western CD's. Trio with Emmylou Harris, Dolly Parton and Linda Ronstadt. Stardust with Willy Nelson and the Nitty Gritty Dirt Band. Jay brought religious music by Piula ALa 'ilima from Hawaii. A harpist music therapist from the hospital visited three times on different days to play lovely melodies. Peggy was pacing and standing a lot. Her cat scan showed that the tumor was unchanged. At least it wasn't bigger.

8/14/99 Peggy in good spirits today. Leroy and Amanda visited. Amanda and I had lunch together Leroy's treat while he stayed upstairs with Peggy. We walked Peggy to the chapel and sang Amazing Grace. We knew all the verses. Leroy gave me 50$ to "grease the skids." Peggy said, "I love you." and hugged Jay and I. She ate about half of her food.

8/15/99 Peg and Bill back from Leavenworth. Carmella, a friend, visited. We went to the beautiful arboretum Japanese Garden. It was tranquil and lovely. Peggy slept peacefully for the entire time I was gone.

8/16/99 Peggy was more alert and coherent and she took lots of naps. It was a very special time spent with Peggy, Peg and Bill. It reminded me of when I was a baby until I was 3 years old when we all lived together in the Kirkland house by the lake. I never thought we would be together again like that. Yet here we were.

8/17/99 With Peg and Bill we went outside to the courtyard and to the chapel. The courtyard was a bit noisy with construction. There were saws and a giant crane.

8/18/99 Peggy slept all day barely waking at mealtimes to eat. She ate less than 1/4th of her food. When asked how she felt about Dr. Goldberg she said, "I love him."

8/19/99 Same as the day before. Father Scot Wright was very

faithful in visiting Peggy when she was in the hospital and offering her the Eucharist. He made the long drive countless times. He prayed for her and with her and anointed her head with oil.

8/20/99 Jay visited. Virginia, Peggy's mother in law, called from Hawaii to tell me how proud she was of me for being so helpful and strong. It was a great encouragement to hear from her. Peggy woke for lunch and ate stew and chowder. Peg and Bill left for Leavenworth. For dinner she ate grapes and drank Enlive enriched juice. She had a sleepy day and I read Crossing Safely by Wallace Stegner. It was a lovely inspiring book about the lives of two couples.

Nick and Laurel Johnson took me out to dinner at a Greek place. The food was excellent and I enjoyed watching the colorful people on Broadway. It was a relief to have a break from the hospital. They were very kind. Nick told me how one of his relatives had died from cancer.

8/21/99 Peggy tore her wound drainage bag off in the early morning. The doctor had punctured her taut abdomen to let some of the excess fluid drain off as it was causing her to be uncomfortable. This procedure was done two times. She drank well and had three "Peggy eggy puddings" and some peach yogurt. She said, "I love you." to Jay. Peggy got up from the bed and said, "I want to go to my house." She was better today in every way. I was so encouraged.

Sunday 8/22/99 Peggy's nurse friend Mary Kay O'Shea came to visit and brought a lovely pot of purple mums. Peg and Bill returned from Leavenworth. I asked Ron the RN to help me understand Peggy's condition. He reviewed her chart then summarized it. Her condition was not improving and he was unsure if she would have any quality time at home left. He was very kind to Peggy. He took beautiful care of her.

Jay visited then came back as Peggy was trying to tell him something. She didn't manage to communicate.

Ron the R.N. discovered that she had been off her thyroid medication since the IL-2 treatments. She ate well and walked to the fish tank room many times. She needed to be guided and fed.

8/23/99 Monday Jean visited. We took Peggy up to the 5th floor room with the view of Mt. Rainier. I'm not sure whether or not she saw it. She seemed to look at me. Jean did go back for her glasses. Then we went to the chapel and sang How Great Thou Art.   Peggy sang along. Peggy put my hand on the statue of Jesus.

Then she had over half of her lunch, napped a bit then went to the fish tank room. She ate a little dinner then woke for Jay's visit to say, "I love you." He said, "I love you infinity."

8/24/99 Peggy was alert and aware. She was up to the potty then up in the chair. She put off her shower to say good bye to me. Peggy said to Peg, "Jen going back to her family." I left for Montana to have 5 days with Seth. While I was gone family friend Ellen came in the afternoons to watch Peggy so Peg and Bill could nap and go for a walk.

While in Montana on August 26th I wrote: Dear Jay and Folks,

I had a very pleasant bus ride home with a bunch of returning college students. It gave me more to write about for my book about riding Greyhound busses.

Brian and I had a nice reunion and Seth arrived a day later by bus from Wyoming. They have movies on their busses. Brian is well. Seth enjoyed swimming lessons and looks forward to soccer. He will be one of the oldest on the team and have a position of responsibility. Seth is busy mastering the computer games and looking forward to an early celebration of his 10th birthday. We got some chocolate cake, fudge frosting and a candle with a one and a zero. We talked to Peggy on the phone and she was clear and called us, "my beloveds". She is doing better today than she was yesterday. It is day by day. I love you all and wish for you all good health and much happiness. Love Jennifer Jaye

Jim White replied August 27th: Dear Jenny,

Good to hear that you had a good trip home and that things are going well there for all of you. It has to be good to get back home again and especially to be with Seth for awhile.

Everyone in Washington is so pleased with your help while you were there and very appreciative as are Gini and I.

Things are calm around here except that we are sorry about your Mom and pray for she and Jay constantly. Of course we are praying also for you and each of the Stark family. It is so tough all the way round. Please take good care and stay strong in the Lord and may God bless you and yours. Jim and Jini

On August 28th Bill went to Leavenworth to get a photographic mural of the Stark kids; Lesley, Willy, Peggy and Jean. It was huge and we propped it on a table at the foot of her bed. Many nurses commented on it especially the Ira Spring photograph of Peggy rappelling down a mountain cliff. Gentle Rose RN kept talking to Peggy about her life and the pictures.

On August 30th Lesley came to the hospital. She brought a lovely shawl that was golden yellow for Peggy.

On August 31st Jon (Peggy's first husband and my father) wrote:
Dear Jennifer,

Further to tonight's phone call. I reiterate that it is very shocking to learn of Peggy's condition. When you go over there to the hospital, mention to her that I feel for her. I will send a card Monday from here. When is Seth going back to Lee in Gillette? And what would he like for a birthday present?

Again give my best regards to Peggy when you see her. Love, Jon

Chapter 31

I returned as soon as I could. I heard that Peggy had been started on hospice care. When asked by the doctor if she wanted to be revived when she died she said, "No." When asked how she felt about death she said, "It will be a great adventure."

9/1/99 to 9/4/99 Long vigil at Peggy's bedside. A very efficient and up beat hospice nurse named Dixie checked in on her daily. Peggy stopped eating and I really missed feeding her. I tried feeding her and Lesley stopped me saying that I wasn't doing it for her but for myself. I started eating her hospital meals. It felt as if I was being nourished by my mother. Brian spoke to her on the phone. I held it up to her ear. He wouldn't tell me what he said. I think he was telling her that she was worthy of a miracle.

There was one night when I slept at her bedside. Lesley slept upstairs at the Inn with Peg and Bill. I slept poorly. There was someone retching across the hallway. Peggy got up many times and I woke each time to assist her to get up to the bathroom. In the morning she tried to get up with the bed rails up. I awoke to her falling over the bed rails across the floor. I called the nurse in a panic. She was fine, mumbling some. It was fortunate that she did not have IV lines in. I felt so bad that she had fallen. They put the restraint vest on as I wasn't sure I would wake up when she tried to get up. She couldn't ask for help. So it was hard to know when she needed help.

On the 1st Peg and Bill left for Leavenworth. When Peg told Peggy that they were going Peggy said, "No!" It was very hard to leave and they hurried back on the 3rd. Family friends Norma and Dick Oxley drove them.

9/4/99 She was comatose this day. We sang songs to her, played music for her and I played my flute. Jay came and left in tears in a hurry. He said that she, "Knew I was there and that I'd said my good-byes." It was a sad day.

Another e-mail on September 4th from Judy Heath Peggy's sister in law reads: I just wanted to call and let you know I am full of love for you and Peggy this morning and sorrow at what you are going through. I called and got through to Lesley and so I have been updated. I am profoundly grateful that Peggy is beyond the agony and the struggle. I do pray to the light that surrounds us all, that you and Peggy, Jennifer and Grandpa Bill and Peg, Lesley, Willy and Jean, Mama and Jim will be eased through the loss.

I tried to tell Peggy when I was there how much I love and admire her. In our teenage years I always admired her physical abilities and her mental talents to the point of feeling awed. She could always out-climb, out-ski, out-read, out-dance, (I can never remember what step comes next) and out-nice me. I have always felt like a tactless cow next to Peggy. Still, I never really felt overshadowed by her because she is always sensitive and kind and funny and accepting. I will miss her quirks of humor, her thoughtful reflections and her stinging satire. The joy she takes in nature is contagious. She has always been so full of love. I was proud of her writing to denounce apartheid. I am glad she got to mother all those many little babies left behind too young by their busy mothers. So many of them received and internalized the comfort of her love and may never know it was she who gave it to them. She has left her beautiful marks on all of us and I will be grateful always for her impact on my life. Love Judy

9/5/99 In the morning Peg called me downstairs to Peggy's room as the nurse Sue had a difficult time finding Peggy's blood pressure. I rested under white cotton blankets in the lounge chair all day listening to Peggy breathe. She had a bed bath and opened her eyes for it but seemed comatose. I told her that I would be OK, that Lesley, Willy and Jean would be there for me. I tried to hold my voice steady as I said this. It was difficult.

Peggy died at 7:20 p.m.. amidst songs, my flute playing and laughter. I started playing Silent Night and I was so nervous that I couldn't get the key right so I tried three different keys. The room filled with laughter as they tried to sing along. Bill and Peg, Lesley and I were with her all day. Near the end Sister Claire the nun, Molly the CNA, and Ron the RN joined us. We sang Ode to Joy. Bill sobbed. Sister Claire said that the song would, "Open the gates of heaven." Bill went downstairs to get dinner and wasn't in the room when she died. It was as if she spared him watching her pass on. Peg and Lesley sang Peggy's special lullaby from childhood. Lesley called Jean and held the phone to Peggy's ear for the last few songs. She died while Peg and Lesley sang Kentucky Babe, another lullaby. She had fast labored breaths for the last few hours of her life. "She sounds as if she is in labor." Someone commented. Ron gave her a shot of pain killer. After she died Ron listened to her chest and confirmed that her heartbeat had stopped. I covered her up with the bright, silky, yellow wrap that Lesley brought from Greece. Lesley placed a small bouquet of cedar berries on her chest. At my request Lesley removed Peggy's wedding ring and gave it to me. She explained what she was doing as she did this. The ring fit on my little finger. Peg and Bill and Lesley spent time in the room with her body. I did not. I helped move things out of the room and bring them upstairs to the Providence Inn. I called Jay and he said he was glad that it was I who let him know. I called my first husband Lee and asked him to tell the news to Seth. Lee said it gave him a pain in his heart. It made me sad that her death was the day before Seth's 10th birthday.

On Monday we composed her obituary, then Lesley and I went to the Bellevue house. Lesley rented a car. We sorted through Peggy's jewelry and selected things for Jean, Peg and Lesley and I. Jay wanted to keep the silver dragon ring. I sorted through her closet and selected some clothes to keep and others to give away to charity.

I wrote an e-mail to Brian: Dear Heart Brian,

We are at Jay's house sorting through my mom's things and finding jewelry and clothes that she would want us to have. We are listening to Beethoven and I am typing to you. We want the memorial service to be on Wednesday but have not received final word yet from the minister. Then after the memorial service I will come home to you in Montana. It will be good to come home to you at long last. Take care, I'll talk to you on the phone real soon. Love always, Jennifer

Jay played Willy Nelson's Angel Flying Too Close To The Ground and went to meditate and cry under a pine tree. I went out to comfort him and he said, "I just don't have anything to say right now." Archbishop Desmond Tutu called and prayed with Jay over the phone. In the evening we went out to a steak house and Lesley treated. She later commented how resilient Jay seemed.

On Tuesday we met with Father Scot Wright to plan the memorial service. Dr. Goldberg saw me in the gift shop of the hospital and said that he heard that Peggy had passed away. He said that she was, "An exceptional person." I got choked up. I wanted to tell him that I wished he had known her when she was well.

The Serrano family visited us at the hospital and brought their delightful little infant son. It was good to see and hold a baby.

On Wednesday we had a memorial service for Peggy at St. John's Episcopal Church in Kirkland. There were lovely flowers from the Sedlocks, The Mehlhoffs, Lesley and other friends. There were fifty people there. Most of the family wore colors. Jay wore a nice blue 3 piece suit. He sat between Lesley and I. Jean was on my other side. Peg and Bill sat alone in front and looked very small as they leaned close to each other for support. Jay cried at the beginning of the service and Jean gave him a tissue with tender gentleness. The family read some of her poems. Then we all formed a circle and shared memories. Then we sang The Happy Wanderer. There was communion and an organist. The final song was Ode to Joy. The pipe organ was large and lovely and filled the back of the church. Father Scot Wright did the service. Nick and Laurel Johnson attended and Nick said to me, "If you can live through this you can survive anything."

Church ladies provided cookies and breads. In the foyer a picture mural of the four Stark kids was on display. Beneath it were the stuffed animals that had been with Peggy in the hospital. The black and white pegasus went to Leavenworth with Peg and Bill. The beanie baby cougar went to Seth. The large Wild Child Bear we later donated to the Washington State Patrol to give comfort to children.

Nick Johnson wrote on September 6: Having known Peggy for a very large part of our lives, (though certainly not as closely as you folks have), we recognize and appreciate the love she had for everyone in her constant quest for peace for all the people of our planet. Perhaps now she can experience the peace she worked so hard to try and coax this world into, and if we all carry some of the love she had with us at all times, we can contribute our small part toward creating peace for some small part of that world. We will love her always, and will always feel her love and peace in our spirit. Bless you all. If you need anything, or would like to talk, or whatever, give us a call or an e-mail or a letter at any time. Nick and Laurel

Rachael wrote on September 13th: Dear Jen,

We heard that your mother passed on. Please accept our condolences and love. I hope you are holding up as well as you can. Her farewell journey sounds wonderful, I hope mine is as lovely and spiritual, I believe that is how it should be. How is Seth doing? Much, much love and empathy. Rachael, Dan and Fiona

On September 17th I wrote to friends: Dear Dan and Diana,

Thank you for your prayers on behalf of my mother. She went to be with her heavenly Father on Sunday, September 5th at 7:20 p.m.. The last days of her life were filled with flowers and music. "It was awful and it was awesome." To quote my aunt Jean. My mother had a lot of grace and love.

Yesterday I had a dream where my mother appeared in front of me bathed in white light and told me that she had overcome the cancer. I got all excited and woke up feeling blessed and joyous.

I will continue to pray for her. Her religion was Episcopal. We had a very special service filled with flowers. In her obituary we suggested that memorials in her name be made to UNICEF. She spent her life working with children and advocating for them. With warm Bahai' greetings from Billings, Jennifer Telander Whitewing

On September 17th Judy Heath wrote: Jenny,

Thank you for sharing your beautiful healing dream of your mother, my friend, Peggy. You have been a golden light for her shining at her side throughout all the dark passage. Your spirit has blessed us all. Each of us is proud of your faith and gentleness. My respect and love for you has deepened and expanded from the general delight I have felt toward you as you grew up. You are a credit to her memory. Love Judy

On September 20th I wrote: Dear Archbishop Desmond Tutu,

On September 16th in the morning I had a dream in which my mother appeared to me and told me how she had overcome the cancer. I awoke feeling refreshed and blessed.

Thank you for writing her all those letters over the years. Your friendship meant a lot to her. Take care, in God's love, Jennifer Telander Whitewing

On September 24th Archbishop Tutu replied: Dearest Jenny,

Peggy was precious and I loved her and looked forward to getting her letters and poems and wonderful news about you. Thank you for sharing your dream. Much love and God's blessings, Desmond Tutu

On September 25th I wrote: Dear Jay and Jim and Jini,

Rosalie Marson, my Native American Shaman friend completed the crossover ceremony for Peggy on September 23rd. She felt that Peggy was reluctant to leave this sphere of existence. She waited by the West door for her every night since her death. On the equinox she was ready. Rosalie said that she dragged a leather box that was very heavy and bound up in ropes. Once she was crossed over there were many helpers (ancestors) who released the ropes and hundreds of lovely white doves flew out free. The ancestors had prepared a banquet table laden with beautiful and abundant food for Peggy's arrival. I thought it was an amazing vision and I just wanted to share it with you. Love always, Jennifer Jaye Telander Whitewing

On September 26 Jay wrote: Dear Dad and Mom,

Things are going OK, with life's usual tribulations. Dear old BOBBIT, could not pass his emissions test necessary to renew license, because he was idling at about 1250 rpm, which is above the 1100 rpm max allowed. The "modern" computer controlled fuel injection has to be retuned on electronic instruments to change the idle speed, beyond my scope. I will do something about it early next week. I am getting a little frustrated with 16 year old car reliability.

I worked 44 hours last week. Things are going OK in that area. My absences over Peggy's Cancer, have had a pediatric effect on Birmingham Steel. They really missed me and seem to have a new found appreciation for my contributions.

The house is very empty and the other side of the bed is too big. These things are looming larger as I fall into a working daily routine. This is to be expected. Since many aspects of life are necessarily different, and I have an almost bewildering array of options, some of which I never expected to have to consider...Gives me quite a bit to think about in my new found spare time. Love you both, Jay

Peggy wrote this poem:

Coming Home
Avalanche lily
High and white on rocks
Catches my breath.
He is there
Like a mountain spring
I drink deep
Never to thirst again.

Chapter 31

"A well kept house is a sign of a wasted life." My mother used to say. The dishes would stack up and the dust would settle. Then she would focus her time and energy on writing. Writing had the highest priority in her life.

"When I die, you will inherit all my writing." she promised. I found computer disks, articles, editorials, poems and letters. Most amazing were the letters. Mother wrote to family, friends, politicians, religious leaders. She advocated for children internationally. Her main passions were the elimination of nuclear war, child abuse prevention, civil rights and the end of apartheid in South Africa.

Once in a grand old log house there lived an old woman who was very tired. She had worked hard all her life. Her eyes saw dimly and she no longer bothered to clean.

Squirrels scampered down from the trees and sneaked into the attic. There they made their nests in the fuzzy insulation. They ran along the rafters and the little ones scurried along the ceiling tiles.

Pigeons nested under the eaves and cooed while they laid their eggs and warmed them with their fat feathery bodies.

Kittens were born to a mother cat in the bedroom. She hid them until their eyes opened then let them explore the room outside the drawer.

Mice discovered food in the kitchen and stowed it away in their nests in the cupboards. They raided the grain bag by nibbling it open and then they raced across the kitchen with a morsel tucked in their cheeks. Beady black eyes peered up fearfully, watching for the cat.

Toads came to sing in the woodpile. On moist spring days they would burrow in the soft dirt at the base of a great pine tree and croak to each other all night long.

A Mother's Gift

"When I die, you will inherit all my poetry and writing." She promised me. When my beloved mother died suddenly of cancer we read her poems at the memorial service and printed one on the program. When my dad offered for me to take her writings home I just couldn't do it, not yet.

A year later we drove out in our big old car and filled the trunk and back seat with her notebooks, letters, scrap books, photo albums and a box of her best shoes. The shoes I mailed to my sister in law as they wore the same size.

"I hope these shoes give your feet years of walking, running, skipping and dancing." I wrote.

Everything else was mine. We took the fireproof safe of important letters

out at my maternal grandparents house. There my grandma sorted the letters from Archbishop Desmond Tutu into years, placing rubber bands around the stacks. They had a correspondence that lasted from 1986 to 1999.

Back home in Montana, in my small apartment I gave away many books and organized shelves to make room for my mother's gift. Gradually I brought boxes in and read through them, organizing the loose papers, newspaper clippings and letters. I tossed out forgotten receipts, grocery lists and school papers. My mother was neither tidy, nor organized. But how she could write. And what courage and determination she had. She wrote advocating on behalf of children all over the world. She wrote to the president, the pope, the queen of England, senators, congressmen, clergy and the newspapers. One of her favorite causes was eliminating the suffering of South African children living under apartheid. That is how she began the correspondence with Archbishop Desmond Tutu.

Besides letters she wrote poetry. Some of it was for family. Some was about the many children she cared for as a teacher. Some was political, especially about civil rights. Her best poems she assembled into books. Her last book was of poems she wrote to archbishop Desmond Tutu. It was entitled Whisper Of Eternity Poems For An Archbishop. Sadly I remember she wanted to be sure to publish it before he died. He had been ill with cancer too. She died first, long before her poems saw print.

The last lucid memory I have of her well was when Brian, Seth and I drove past her home. We considered going to Snoqualmie falls before stopping by. But she appeared, looking for us. She could sense we were there. So we stopped, went in and ate the tomatoes and artichokes she had laid out for us. We had been to a family re-union. She had not felt well enough to sit in the car for 4 hours to get to the coast. We missed her. By the same time next year she was dead.

In the hospital she had surgery and a grapefruit sized widespread cancer called melanoma was discovered in her abdomen. So they moved her to the cancer ward where she had one series of Inter-leukin-2 and that nearly killed her with fevers spiking at 106 and delirium that persisted the rest of her life. After the fever I rushed to her bedside from Montana to Washington and braided purple orchids in her hair.

Chapter 32

After The Custody Battle

My first husband and I had a stormy four year marriage followed by a divorce and custody battle nearly as long as the marriage. We have one son. The arrangement ended up as joint custody with Lee having primary physical custody and me having frequent visitation.

I did not want it this way. I do not like it. But what matters is that it works. Our son is doing fine.   His well being is more important than his parent's power struggles.

We separated when our son Seth was 3. During that time Seth lived with his father 4 days per week and me 3 days per week. This was based on my work schedule, not on parenting ability. Then Lee moved. I followed 150 miles away, settling in a strange city I didn't want to live in just to be near Seth.

We fought in the courts until we ran out of time and money. Then Lee moved again. Visitation was mediated in the courts and I remember driving 100 miles across the frozen wind swept praries of Montana to rendezvous with Lee and Seth every other weekend. It was a stressful and hazardous drive when the ice lay on the road in sheets and the blizzards blew. Seth adjusted well to all the travelling. He slept in the car or played games.

When school started for Seth he needed some stability. So he visited me on vacations. Lee moved with Seth three more times. I did not follow them as Lee told me the moves were temporary. Also there were no work opportunities for me in the remote towns.

When you create a child with someone it is a permanent bond. Memories of our lawyers have faded. They helped us to set up rules and they helped themselves to our money. The lawyers don't matter anymore.

All that remains is the best interests of the child Seth. We don't argue anymore. We discuss. We negotiate. We discuss Seth's activities and progress and we negotiate visitation. On major holidays Lee and I alternate having our only son.

Sometimes I am ashamed that I don't have custody of my son.

Oftentimes I try to avoid telling acquaintances about my situation. Always I miss him. I call him several times a week and he calls back. I try to write him a letter or a post card every day. Seth saves the post cards. It is fun to send him new and educational ones. He rarely answers the letters. He says he is too busy. At least I get cards from Seth on major holidays like Mother's Day and my birthday.

Valentines' Day is bittersweet to me. It was the day the court appointed guardian ad litum decided that Seth would be better off with his father than with me. I presented her with positive information about myself and my family. Lee presented her with negative information about me. He got all his army buddies to write derogatory statements. She believed the evidence as it was presented to her. After all these years I have forgiven her. Still my life with my son moving away from me all the time has been very difficult.

When he visits it is a joyful homecoming. We have a celebration, a party. I indulge him. I take him to all the latest movies and amusement parks. I buy him fresh berries and whipped cream even when they are costly. The grocery bill jumps up 50%. I take time off from work to be with him. I am making up for lost time. The days of his childhood are fleeting and I love him so.

Seth is 11 now. He does very well in school and enjoys soccer, wrestling, piano, percussion and Boy Scouts when he is with Lee. Lee is a dedicated father who is involved is Seth's activities. When he visits me Seth relaxes, plays computer games, watches movies and is working on his first action adventure fantasy novel on the word processor.

"He is a blessing." Lee once said. On this we agree. In fact we find a lot to agree on these days. Pleasant, humorous e-mails are exchanged. I pay child support every month. Lee and I negotiate visitation with tact and diplomacy and always compromise in Seth's best interest.

Lee is good at providing structure for Seth. I am good at letting Seth be spontaneous. Our co-parenting succeeds where our marriage failed. And we all benefit. Life is good!

Angel Mother

Mother tried to save the world
And was herself
saved

The innocent lives she blessed
With gentle care
thrived

The man she loved
Stayed by her side until
death

Her spirit soared to freedom
Of divine
view

To look below to
Loved ones toiling on
earth

Enfolded in her
Gentle wings they
know

Her infinite love
And kind grace
flows

In streams of light, flowers grow
Come springtime in the
mountains

Chapter 33

A list for the family trek to the Enchantment Laked when Seth was 12:
Sleeping bag, Seth
Sleeping pad, Jen
Sleeping pad, Seth
Tent
Pack, Jen
Pack, Seth
Day pack or packs?
Boots, Jen
Boots, Seth
Socks, heavy, Jen (how many)
Socks, heavy, Seth   "
Socks, lite, Jen
Socks, lite, Seth
Parka, water resistant, Jen
Parka, water resistant, Seth
Poncho, Jen
Poncho, Seth
Down jacket? Jen
Down jacket? Seth
Sweater (or similar warmth) Jen
Sweater (ditto) Seth
Warm shirt Jen
Warm shirt Set
Tee shirt(s?) or tank(s), Jen
Tee shirt(s?) or tank(s), Seth
Long pants (decide what kind) Jen
Long pants (decide what kind) Seth
Shorts, Jen
Shorts, Seth
Underwear, Jen
Underwear, Seth

Long underwear? Jen
Long underwear? Seth
Hat, Jen
Hat, Seth
Gloves, Jen
Gloves, Seth
Knife
Sunscreen
Dark glasses, Jen
Dark glasses, Seth
Tooth brush, Jen
Tooth brush, Seth
Toothpaste
Water bottles, Jen
Water bottles, Seth
Flashlights, 2
Bug dope
Spoons, 2
Cups, 2
Map

Stove & gas   Use Lesley & Tom's
Water filter

FOOD
6 dinners
Dinner dessert?
6 breakfasts (what? List:)
7 lunches (what? List:)
Trail food (gorp, nuts, etc.)

A bitch about Sleeping Lady Mountain Retreat downsizing. And in the process of writing my thoughts take form into a letter. And the letter says Help! How can I be a gracious, loving, giving person in this place? On the way home I hear Hey! You've got to hide your love away. By The Beatles. It feels like that. So many good people cut. No security for long term employees. No mercy for accident victims. Steely magnolias who I fear and admire. Avoiding the swing of the ax daily. Only partial reassurances. Destabilizing forces. Hard to know what will happen. Nancy mad at changes. Arguing over uniforms. We're all expendable. Caring yet detaching. No politics. Avoiding knowing too much yet feeling everything. New people all over..... all female. I fear and my fight or flight impulse comes and goes. They work me full time yet offer me no benefits. I prefer part time. My real work is elsewhere. I invoke the spirit of the land and the spirit of father O'Grady for protection. I will not become an indifferent elitist. I work there but they don't have my loyalties. They offer nothing for loyalty. I just want to get a cell phone and get in the car and drive.........

"I was going to cook some pierogies and Uncle Uli's meatballs to serve when you'd reached a point in your writing where you wanted to stop. So you've reached a point in your writing where you don't want to begin!"

"So you think writing would be a good idea?"

"It might help."

"What should I write about?"

"In my book are four natural modes of expression; catharsis, description, free intuitive and reflection."

" You are so good to me."

"That's funny I thought that you were thinking, 'She's mad at me for making her write.' Like I was some kind of writing teacher."

The music of Hildegard Von Bingen is playing on the stereo. The breeze outside rushes through the budding trees and the pines drop their old cones. The light is blank white with a high overcast like a pale sheet over the sun.

Earlier we took a walk to the river with our dog friend joining us for part of the journey. She likes to stop in the road and wait for us to come back. Today she didn't. Today she just disappeared into someone's yard then she greeted us as we returned. We call her the Bratwurst of Love. She is part beagle and part something else. She has grey and white thick medium length fur. Bratwurst has symmetry on the fur on her face and lines between her eyes.

"What ya thinkin' about?"

"A little bit about Hilda?"

"Would you rather write about one of your people?"

"I think not."

Only makes me think how I didn't love them enough.

I feel blank like the sky. I feel like there is no cure for this blankness, this isolated feeling. Brian is here and he is warm and loving. He keeps playing beautiful music. Now it is Moby- God moving over the face of the waters.

This music makes me think of the waves of the ocean in the wind with the light breaking through the clouds and descending on the sea. It starts and swells with little repeating notes like ripples and symbols crashing like surf and resonance like the majesty of God.

Chapter 34

I was a home health aid for 3 years then a certified Nurses Aid for 1. Of all my home health clients Tom was the most memorable. Here is my take on his story.

Tom

Once while caring for Tom I found myself in his basement surrounded by wheelchairs that had belonged to his dead brothers. The different sizes of chairs told silent tales about the occupants. They all suffered and died from muscular dystrophy. Three brothers in one family died. Tom held on the longest.

When I first met him I saw his small twisted frame laying in his bed. He had a feeding tube going into his stomach, an oxygen canula going into his nose and he was connected to a ventilator by a tracheotomy opening in his neck. That made three kinds of life support keeping him alive. He required around the clock care and this was done in his parent's home.

He was 26 and had been a normal little boy once. Then the disease first crippled him landing him in a wheelchair as his feet pointed down and legs bowed. His muscles were rigid and stiff and contorted. His back bent with both kyphosis and lordosis--two directions of spinal curvature.

Then muscular dystrophy weakened his muscles so he had minimal strength to breath or cough. Tom was connected to a ventilator all night and some days. When he breathed on his own he had to be monitored. As he couldn't cough, he choked on his own mucus. Secretions flowed into his lungs and he needed to be suctioned. This was done by his nurses or his mother with me assisting. Suctioning was done as needed on demand. It involved disconnecting the tracheotomy tube and squirting sterile saline solution down the opening in his neck then vacuuming up the mucus and secretions from his trachea with a plastic canula. During this procedure Tom couldn't talk and had to trust his care givers as he was helpless and couldn't breathe. The intense look in his eyes was heartrending.

As Tom passed his time he would sit in bed or in his wheelchair with his TV remote control on his tray or table and a plastic mouth suctioning wand in his hand. He would vacuum the secretions out of his mouth since he lacked the strength to swallow and cough. The secretions traveled through a plastic tube to a clear plastic box on a bedside table. At least once a day I would empty this vat of spittle into the toilet and wash the box and rinse the tubing. It smelled terrible. The other thing that Tom was able to do for himself with his hands was to get his penis out from his sweat pants flap so he could pee into the hand held plastic urinal. Someone had to hold the urinal for him. So he had no privacy.

Liquid food was pumped slowly into his stomach through a hole in his abdomen. We added green dye to the white milky food so we could tell if it started to leak. Medicines were added to his food in liquid or powdered form. An electric pump hummed and moved the green liquid food into his stomach. This was because he had lost the strength and muscle control to swallow. We cleaned the area around the wound daily.

Tom lived in a suburban home with his parents. He had a comfortable bedroom with an electric hospital bed in it that faced an entertainment center made of oak with a large screened TV on it. That TV was Tom's window to the world. He watched soap operas and got involved with the characters in his mind. He was critical of their beauty which always struck me as ironic.

In the six months that I cared for Tom, I learned more than I wanted to know about his family. His father was a trucker, who smoked cigars and referred to my supervising RN as "A douche bag." He was bitter that his son was ill and that the other two had died. So like many family members of patients he raged at the nurses and "the system". Although I was in the home 6 hours a day, I was an outsider.

Tom's mother looked forward to times when he was on the road earning money and not at home underfoot. She dedicated most of her time and energy caring for her son. She would defend him from people who disparaged his prognosis. She took charge and mastered complex medical procedures to help care for him at home. She worked herself to exhaustion and drew strength from her faith.

The ventilator and oxygen concentrator machines had back up generators in case of power outage that took up considerable space in the bedroom where Tom spent most of his life.

Some rare days his father would lift him gently with strength and patient kindness out of his bed and into his electric wheelchair for a few hours. Tom could go down the hall and across the living room with his cords and tubes trailing behind him to gaze out the window at the quiet street. I thought he had a wistful look as he wondered at the world beyond. A world that he could only travel in via ambulance to a hospital. His family tried to keep him home, where he was comfortable and surrounded by love.

The home was clean and pleasant. Fran was a good housekeeper. There was a funny fat wiener dog who came in and out. Everything seemed very middle class and normal except for the back bedroom.

His mother Fran dedicated herself to him and the filling out of extensive documents needed to finance his care through Medicaid. When we were wiping Tom after a bowel movement his parents referred to this as, "Doing the paperwork." Such humor helped keep everyone sane under the stress. She was a homemaker and mother who had six children and her three sons had muscular dystrophy. Two had died in childhood but Tom held on and lived in a state of dependence on machines and life support into his 20's. It was a long life for someone with this diagnosis.

Tom never had the experience of growing up. As he grew he became more ill and more dependant. He had no future family of his own to look forward to. Aside from his mother and sisters, his nurses were the only women in his life. He expressed these losses and longings by sexually harassing the nurses. Maybe he learned it from his father. I remember his father calling me "a bedpan queen." Tom would comment on the physical attributes of the models and actresses on TV. Then he would compare me to them and insult me for not measuring up. His insults were subtle and pervasive. I tried to ignore them with a mixed sense of pity and duty.

On the walls in his bedroom were mementos from the fire department's muscular dystrophy summer camps Tom had attended in the past. He still had friends in the fire department, firemen would occasionally call.

On Valentine's day Tom received valentines from his nurses. For one licensed practical nurse he was her only patient as he needed 40 hours per week of care. She decorated the plastic boxes his wipes came in and gave them as gifts. Years after I had finished my work at Tom's house I saw that nurse at a restaurant and she was still caring for him at home. He was still alive! She still made her career caring for only him.

Occasionally his sisters and nieces and nephews would visit. I wondered if his cute little blond nephew would get muscular dystrophy or if Tom had once looked like him before the disease struck.

Tom had a patient personality. He was able to get what he needed from his caregivers and his parents through persuasion rather than demands.

Tom valued life and struggled for it. Some days he struggled for every breath. I found myself holding my breath while in his room as if his dissonant biorhythms were altering my own.

Tom told me he was hoping for a cure. He was holding onto life in hopes for a cure. I promised to study about muscular dystrophy when I returned to college. I wanted to find a cure too.

Quads in Cowboy Boots

Montana quadriplegic men, although they have limited mobility and sensation and need home health care, still wear cowboy boots.

I would arrive and let myself in to find my patient waiting in bed for assistance. Sometimes we lifted them into their electric wheelchairs. Sometimes we used a mechanical Hoyer lift.

The best time we ever had was with a electrical hoist that moved him out of the bed, over the chair then into the chair with a mouth control. All that remained was to help in the shower and get him dressed for work where he was a grain buyer. The cowboy boots were hard to get on his limp feet. But they were important. Boots bring self respect.

Being paralyzed is one of the most trying afflictions. Yet people have different ways of handling it. One quad I met not because he needed a home health aid, but because he worked for an agency that counseled the handicapped. He drove a van to work and truly celebrated life. He had been paralyzed young in a motorcycle accident. His boots had big straps and he pulled them on himself. Very self reliant and self actualizing.

One Native American man who was a quad had experienced abandonment by his family and tribe. They viewed him as dead. He suffered greatly, smoked marijuana and drank beer long into the night. I was only at his apartment once. He had a friend over. I helped him to bed then the friend asked for help too. I was unprepared for the friends missing body parts. There were simply NO LEGS and it seemed no lower abdomen and back. He said he was, " Grateful to have a professional like you help me." I felt respected and valued, though confused.

My favorite quad in cowboy boots was Harry. Harry was once stranded in bed for 4 days with no home health aid and no way to call for help on the phone. He told me how he chewed his catheter so the urine wouldn't back up and kill him and how he moved around and struggled to sit up so he could still breathe. (Quads sometimes have trouble breathing in the prone position due to poor muscle tone.) Somehow he survived.

Harry had concerns like sores on his legs and feet and slow bowels that required the help of the visiting RN. After the indignity and the awful stench of the bowel program it was time for his shower. Harry loved his hot showers. He had some movement in his arms but no ability to grasp with his hands. So he had me stand in the shower with him and scrub his scalp in circles with a scalp brush. "Clockwise! Bigger circles! Now over the ear. Not in the ear damn you!"

For breakfast starters there was pills, vitamins and beer. Once in his electric wheelchair Harry could get around quite well and be a large and powerful somewhat ornery man. He frequently slammed into furniture and walls with his wheelchair. "Where the hell's my cowboy hat?" He wore a white one, extra tall in the summer. I have this theory that good guys wear white hats and bad guys wear black. Old myths.

He had me water his plants. "More water." I flooded the Norfolk pine and he liked it. The thing had a gangly green presence. Then go shopping for necessities like beer and cigarettes. Harry was a likeable guy with a heart of gold but a real aggressive type A. Harry enjoyed life and loved his grown son and daughter. I think he lived for the joy of seeing them. He never spoke of his wife, or former wife.

I cared for Harry for a long time. He really preferred to do for himself. I wondered if a well trained monkey would have served him better! Still he remained friends with many people including his nurses and home health aids.

Love and Alzheimers

"If we live long enough, we're all going to get it." Dr Rowe MD Neurologist.

At the nursing home I worked all the wings. Since I wanted to be a medical professional they threw me to the fire and expected me to care for everyone, all shifts and some doubles which were 16 hours. Most wondrous and terrifying was C wing the locked down Alzheimer's unit.

"You have to have a safe zone." Carolyn the RN told me. "A place where you can avoid attack, because you can't fight with them. That's elder abuse. No matter what don't get into a fight."

During day shift the staff was 2 CNA's, a LPN and a supervisor RN. At night there was only one CNA. "Days like this only get riper." The head CNA said ruefully. Everyone needed to get up, dressed, bathed and ready for breakfast or an outing.. Relatives, especially loyal spouses, came and went. Some folks could dress themselves some couldn't move.

Cecelia got up and dressed herself, wearing extra plastic beads and sometimes she would put layer upon layer of clothing on herself. She would put bras and panties on the outside of her clothing. So we'd stifle a giggle and take her gently by the hand and assist her back to her room and help her dress normally. Then she'd go find her "husband." Both Cecelia and Dale had lost their spouses. But in the small world of C wing they had found each other and love, and thought they'd been together always. Much fuss was made about keeping them apart. But they snuck around and we found them making love often.

After Ralph's wife passed away. He was beside himself and tried to escape the nursing home. So he ended up in C-Wing although I never thought he had Alzheimer's. He used to ask me for work. He wanted to help so I gave him a small towel and asked him to polish the wooden rail. He took great pride in being useful.

He fell for Cecelia and I found her in his bed. He was very happy. Except Dale and Ralph had some concept of what was going down. Cecelia blissfully sneaked off with both of them. She may not have realized what she was doing. There is a sort of innocence to Alzheimer's. Once the rivalry led to yelling and blows.

A very dear lady named Ella resided in the last room near the high fenced courtyard. She talked constantly and made no sense. Her unintelligible babble was pleasant like the sound of geese. Very tactile, Ella loved to embrace and be walked up and down the hall by her arm.

Dirk was dangerous and had been a wife batterer and an oilman in his younger days. He could really swing his fists. Dirk didn't appreciate the help we provided, especially the diapering. It was a dirty dangerous job for two CNA's. Still I once got socked in the gut, hard. His lovely loyal attractive wife visited daily. Yet she stayed just out of reach.

Glen wore diapers only at night. And when I would go in to change him I was alone. So who would believe me when I say he thrice proposed marriage? "Madam will you marry me?" He'd ask while reaching for my hand and looking into my eyes. Maybe it doesn't count for real in the middle of the night, in an Alzheimer's unit during a diaper change, but I was charmed.

Mealtimes were really scary. The noise level would build and food would get slopped everywhere, even thrown. The elders wore terry cloth bibs which they tore off. The soft mashed foods were appetizingly formed into familiar shapes as part of the Dining With Dignity program. For example, pureed foods were poured into molds or shaped with pastry bags. By the end of the meal it would be a mess anyway. Trays were hurled to the floor, plastic cups of grape juice dribbled across the floor. Clothes would need to be changed and faces and hands wiped.

Zella was end stage Alzheimer's and had mobility only in her right arm and her fingers formed a sort of claw. She absent mindedly pecked and scratched at us as we fed and bathed her. "Don't let her hook you." One CNA warned me. "She won't let go."

"YOU YOU YOU YOU YOU YOU YOU YOU YOU YOU!" Penny the retired postmistress would say as I came into her room. She really didn't like being turned or having her diaper changed. "YOU YOU YOU YOU YOU YOU!" She'd say accusingly. I felt so mean, yet I knew she needed help whether she understood or not.

Bertha had a tatoo on her wrist. She had survived a concentration camp in Nazi Germany and now relived the terror the way most people relive their memories from youth. She'd wake drenched in sweat and screaming in terror. "They are coming for us. The Nazi's are going to shoot all of us." She would accept reassurance and comfort. She called nurses "Jeanie." "Jeanie it is time to run. Hide now. Be quiet. Oh Jeanie I thought I'd never see you again. Jeanie I love you." I never did find out who Jeanie was. I was glad to be Jeanie for her. Jeanie brought such comfort. Maybe Jeanie was her sister. Bertha had nightmares and flashbacks. Was it post traumatic shock syndrome? That and Alzheimer's. Bertha was a dear woman. We all comforted her as creatively as we could, taking her for walks in the sunshine so she could feel free. But she never outran the Nazi's in her mind. She outlived them but the memories were a wound like the numbers on her wrist.

Loren had a little old home next to the refinery and a family of 8 grown kids to look after her. They occasionally needed a Personal Care Attendant to stay with her. I spent the night several times. It was a 12 hour shift. OK to sleep as long as you could leap out of bed and keep watch over her if she needed to get up. We dead bolted the doors so she wouldn't wander out into the snow. We took the knobs off of the gas range so she wouldn't burn herself or start a fire.

In the wee hours of the morning she was up. I went to her and she wanted me to kneel and pray with her, "God have mercy on us poor widows." She was in danger of falling so I assisted her to the bathroom. By the time I got her settled down again it was dawn. She enjoyed her family and doing simple puzzles, games and coloring in a coloring book. Her loyal family and the home health agency kept her in her own home with 24 hour a day 7 day a week supervision until she died. It was great to be a part of that kind of loyal love.

Karmic paybacks are hell. My great uncle had a long distinguished career as a forensic psychiatrist in the prison system. Then he retired, enjoying his farm and burgeoning family of 10 kids and their kids and the great grandkids. Then the madness set in. At first it was manageable at home with family helping.

"Dad's so unabashed. He's happy to sing at the top of his lungs. He never sang before in his life!" Eldest daughter Karma told me. When I visited I remember his delight at his spoiled obese flatulent cows. He would roar with mirth as they trotted off farting in step.

After several years he started getting more confused. He'd wander off and get lost. The last straw was when he threatened to kill his wife. She put him into a nursing home Alzheimer's unit. There he flirted with the ladies. His memories, even of family members gradually slipped away. The whole damn situation was and is unnerving to my grandfather, his older brother.

You Follow Your Heart
Death and Loss

The home was filthy as we entered during a time of crisis. My task was to watch the babies while a meeting took place. The voices in the other room raised with intensity as I struggled to keep the babies quiet. One was well nourished and just a little fussy. His cousin was pale and malnourished. His cries tugged at my heart. I prayed for guidance.

The babies' mothers were young and single. The great grandmother had died. The only man of the house, the great grandfather was frail but determined. The grandmother had terminal cancer and was home to die. The littlest baby's mother was only 16.

Another volunteer came from the other room to help with the

healthier cousin. I focussed my attention on little Don. I observed his young mother yell at him then play with him, roughly.

I'm not sure what went down at the meeting. I did talk to someone about my concerns for little Don. He seemed dehydrated, weak, small and his mother was overwhelmed with her own mom dying.

Later I visited the mom in the hospital and helped her dial long distance to her daughter in California. I spoke frankly about their tense family situation to the charge nurse and she was placed in a nursing home for her final weeks.

Little Don, his young mother and great grandfather seemed OK at the funeral. I came by several times to bring food. Don grew into a lively toddler. Then his mother got depressed. I gave her a colorful Mexican blanket. She was suicidal and she lost Don to the foster care system. It broke his great grandfather's heart.

There was hope that little Don could be kept in the family. There were sisters. That fell through. His foster family ended up adopting him. They sent pictures and let him talk to his great grandpa. "I love you babba." He said.

The great grandpa was hopeful that he could be raised by people of the same faith. This was not possible. Then again trust and love abide. I remember the mom telling me with pride how her daughter wanted to keep the baby, despite being raped. "She made a brave choice." In giving him up under duress I think she made another brave choice.

___Jennifer J. T. Whitewing

Earnest Love

Paralyzed by a stroke, Earnest Love lay moaning, prone in a bed in the nursing home. His legs were still and so was his right arm. His left arm, fingers curled into a fist flailed out and hit the nurses when they came near.

A tube fed him white food solution through a hole in his abdomen as he couldn't swallow food.

The first time I went into his room to change his diaper and re-position him I was shocked at the size of his left testicle. It was the size of a football! He had a hernia, a loop of intestine that had slipped through a muscle wall and descended into his testicle. Every new nurse aide would see this and go immediately to report to the head nurse. She told us that one day it would simply explode which did little to reassure us. We would cleanse him gently, replace the diaper and pad that covered the hernia and reposition him in bed.

"One two three, LIFT!" We would move him up in the bed then roll him to the right, left or center and carefully place rolled pillows under the soft pad and draw sheet. If needed we would change all his bedding by making half the bed lengthwise then rolling him over onto the clean sheets and taking away the soiled sheets, smoothing the clean ones out then repositioning him. Earnie would look at us with fear and confusion in his eyes and flail with his arm. One aid said he was thinking, "Oh God, here they come again."

Breathing treatments were given with a mask and oxygen with water vapor and medication. The LPN's always administered those

On the TV above the bed we played the Country and Western dance music station. He had enjoyed that kind of music before his stroke. It was unclear whether he enjoyed it, but we had to try to make life better for him.

He moaned constantly, his moans turning to yells when he was being tended to. It was eerie to hear him. I felt that I was part of a system that kept him in this state of flux between life and death and it seemed cruel.

His family never visited him. One niece told me, "I want to remember Uncle Earnie as he was when he was healthy." In their absence many decisions were made by the nursing home administrators regarding his care.

For many years he lived like this.

Twice weekly there was a stretcher on a sturdy frame that wheeled over to his bed and the bath aide would lower it to the level of the bed and transfer him onto it for a ride down the hallway to the big bathtub. The stretcher would lower smoothly into the warm bathwater then lift him up dripping wet when the bath was done.

Then the aide would cover him with towels to dry him then a sheet for the ride back to the bed.

Most residents enjoyed their bath. Earnest Love just moaned faster.

Good Seizure Girl

Her grandmothers desperate dedication and enduring heart-breaking love were evident to all schedulers at the office. Still no one wanted to stay in the position and help out Kimberly. Why?

Kimberly's special ed bus dropped her off as I waited outside for her at her grandparent's house. We went out to wheel her up the ramp into the house. She was strapped into he wheelchair at the waist, ankles and wrists. Also there were plastic braces on her legs and a body brace on her back, with bosoms molded into the front.

First thing we took her to her bedroom and gently removed all the braces and changed her diaper, then gave her a bath. At 15 she was normal size and proportion, and pretty. But Oh God! Her seizures. Even with high doses of barbiturates and other meds she had seizures frequently, continually and violently. As I carried her to the bath she had a grand mal. It wasn't unusual or even remarkable. It was tragic.

She was helpless as an infant or maybe even more so. She couldn't grasp anything, feed herself or even swallow properly. Meals were tiny spoonfuls of soft foods gently and patiently fed to her between seizures. Pills of every color got ground up and mixed into the soft foods. Grandma would say, "Good girl." It made me very sad. The strain of taking care of her had been too much for her parents so the task had gone to her grandparents. It was slowly killing them. They were dying, each of them of different kinds of cancer. Death hung over the house. Yet love was there too. A desperate faithful kind of love.

"Kimberly would be a real character if she didn't have these seizures." grandma claimed with a tinge of tragic hope.

On the walls of her bright, clean bedroom were projects and awards from special ed at school. It was evident that they were for building self esteem and self concept. "Kimberly Really Tried Today."

"Kimberly Was A Good Helper Today." In her condition she was unable to interact, communicate, learn or achieve. She couldn't talk, crawl, feed herself or go to the bathroom. The state was obligated to educate her for 6 hours every school day even if that meant feeding her, medicating her and changing her diapers. I guess they had time to write up certificates about her and I guess that was good since it made her grandparents feel good enough to post them on her wall.

As I puzzled over this we laid her on her bed, took her out of her plastic body braces and turned on the TV to cartoons. Her eyes didn't focus or track and she had more seizures. I wondered if these routines were soothing or if she could notice.

Grandma provided a closet of clean, comfortable, custom made clothes and soft slippers. Her clean tennis shoes never touched the ground and were the latest styles. They only got strapped to the pedals of the wheelchair.

The work for the home health care aid took four hours a day. Grandma had exacting standards as evidenced by the tidy house and lovely yard. Yet she just couldn't lift Kimberly, bathe her or manage the household and take care of her. It was overwhelming.

I only helped a few times. Every seizure I felt Kimberly struggling to die and I wondered at the "love" that maintained her in this state of vegetative, drugged catatonia. I never heard what happened to Kimberly after her grandparents died of their breast and bladder cancers.

Caring for Hilda made me realize how much I wanted to care for Seth and Nanny. This is her "story" as I wrote it

Hilda

"Help me! I need help! Hilda cried out. She was in a very elegant assisted living community called The Vista when I met her. She called out for help so they asked me to volunteer to be near her and keep her company as the nurses were not able to attend to her at all times. Her apartment was very nice with antiques and figurines and seasonal decorations and angels. The afternoon I met her she was crying. I kept her company and distracted her from her pain.

She enjoyed being pushed around in her wheelchair and she

enjoyed visiting people, animals and seeing art at St John's Lutheran home. Hilda liked the white doves that cooed softly and the velvety soft brown rabbit named Hershey. She admired the cats and petted the gentle golden retriever.

Hilda had very refined manners and was a gentlewoman. She would say things to me like, " And if you come to visit me again, I would be most pleased." Her mind was sharp but she needed help.

Once we visited the Center For The Generations and parked her wheelchair in the midst of the three year olds. She delighted in the children. I told the children that Hilda was a grandma and that she had been a teacher. One saucy little boy said, "But now she doesn't do anything." Her pace was so much slower than the children. I told him that she was retired after working hard all her life and now she had time to rest. The boy told us wistfully how his mother had to work.

I looked forward to volunteering with Hilda. We would go to see the geese and ducks if the weather was fine. As we moved up and down the long hallways we admired the decorations. Hilda was particularly fond of the angels.

Several times I took her to where church services were being held. It touched my heart that her favorite hymn was How Great Thou Art. That had been my late mother's favorite hymn too.

Hilda liked seeing the cats, dogs, birds and rabbits at St. John's. As she needed more help she moved across the street from the Vista to St John's Lutheran Home. The move seemed to make her sad. I know she was fond of residents and nurses at the Vista. Also she moved into a smaller space and had to lose some of her possessions.

I remember her lovely daughter in law coming to clean and decorate the room. She was gracious and kind and asked me to stay though I offered to leave since space was limited and I thought they might need some family time.

At the end of my afternoon visits I would wheel Hilda down to the dining room. It was a beautiful room with expansive windows, a view of the mountains and large living plants. The aids walked and wheeled the residents in and dinner was served.

More than once people asked if I was Hilda's granddaughter. I always replied that I was her friend. Since that was what Joan the Reverend said Hilda needed. It made me miss my own grandmother intently. When my husband left his job we decided to move to be near my elderly grandparents. I didn't say goodbye to Hilda. I just sort of disappeared. Maybe volunteering to be with Hilda got me in touch with the longings of my heart.

Reverend Joan wrote me to tell me Hilda passed away suddenly. I see her now as a glorious and gracious kindly angel. I am glad she was in my life and I in hers.

Littly Poochie and Leena

Leena lived in a nice home with her daughter and son in law. She was strong in mind and spirit and just needed a little help getting going in the mornings. Pretty wonderful for 95 years old.

She was well mannered and soft spoken and it was easy to be gentle and patient with her. The loss of her life was when her husband died. Often she spoke about him and their lives together. "We raised our kids, then the grandkids came." It is hard to outlive loved ones, especially one's mate.

Leena would walk slowly with my assistance to the kitchen where I'd prepare her a simple breakfast. She loved citrus fruit and wheat toast. I paid attention to Leena, what she ate and what she said, because she was in great shape and had a clear mind and a sweet spirit. A life well lived. A long life worth living still.

After breakfast on fine spring days when the weather was mild and breezy we'd go outside to the garden. Then I'd bring my long haired Chihuahua Gizmo to visit her. "Littly Poochie!" She called him. He was a gentle affectionate creature who came along with me as I helped clients. He enjoyed them and they enjoyed him no one more so than Leena. He stood on his hind legs and pawed her knees. He was a tiny dog.

All was not rosy in the home. Leenas daughter was a high pressure real estate agent and she was overwhelmed. Sometimes she'd threaten to put Leena in a nursing home. One day I asked Leena about a bruise on her wrist and she tried to shush me. Her daughter heard my question and she started yelling about it. I never did figure out what was up. Even a good life has its tragic moments where everything seems ready to break.

Nadia's Unattainable Dream

Born with no hands or feet and only stumps for arms and legs, Nadia edured incredulous stares wherever she went. The last time I saw her, she was lost in the elevator at the Four Seasons Olympic Hotel. She appeared in the bustling kitchen in her wheelchair. She was job hunting. I introduced myself as an old acquaintance from Junior High School and showed her the way to the personnel office. The perfectly proportioned tall blonde personnel director was openly aghast. Nadia didn't get a job. Not that day. Not in that four star hotel.

Nadia's parents prepared a slide show about her for her school mates. In it she was introduced as a human being not a handicapped person. We were advised to stare at the slideshow so that when she came to school and wheeled down the halls in her electric wheelchair we would not stare at her. Still we stared, if only surreptitiously behind her back.

Being born with no arms or legs is a rare birth defect. There was another boy near Nadia's age with the same condition. Somewhere. I hoped that they would meet and be friends.

Nadia wore prosthesis, artificial arms and legs. This made her appear more normal. Still she needed an electric wheelchair, except for the times she'd race across the tile floor on her stumps. Usually Nadia won these races against kids on their knees. The stumps were all asymmetrical which was another cruel irony.

In order to write Nadia held a pen or pencil between her longest arm stump and her cheek and manipulated the writing implement with her tongue, facial muscles and arm stump. A tote bag or back pack hung from the back of her electric wheelchair. Often I saw buddies carrying her books for her.

Using the bathroom was very time consuming. Passing time between classes was only 5 minutes. Nadia went in during class time for privacy. She had to transfer from chair to toilet then back. I never fully understood how she managed to wipe. It occurred to me that her artificial legs might have gotten in the way of the whole proceeding, and been heavy too.

Nadia's parents and siblings encouraged her to have a full, normal life. She was an exemplary citizen who even volunteered doing phone work for the community. I guess that is why she thought she could work at the fanciest hotel in Seattle. I wanted her to get the job. Instead she had no chance. The first impression was just too startling for the perfect barbie princess in charge of personnel.

Rhoda

Rhoda loved her dogs. Twenty-seven of them. Caring for her and her son meant caring for her kennel as well. In the early summer mornings I'd walk across the yard to the barn where the dogs were kenneled. First I'd measure kibble into the bowls of the tiny long haired chihuahuas then set them free in their yard after they gobbled their chow. Then I'd feed the shelties even the ones that tried to nip me and set them free in the other two yards. Then I'd feed the white long haired Akita with the sparkling black nose who lived on a chain in the front yard. After the dogs it was time to tend to pregnant Rhoda and her 3 year old son Ryan.

Before abandoning the family the husband bought an expensive red sports car. Then he drove from Montana to California. To his credit he did send money.

Rhoda's doctors ordered her on bed rest for the last trimester of her pregnancy. She could get up to the bathroom, but no more. She had a history of five late term miscarriages.

I moved into her home to help. My son was her son's age and we met at church. Ryan was a beautiful child with blonde curly locks and a gleam in his eye. Little Ryan went to daycare at first then got so violent he was expelled. He thought I had made his daddy go away. It seemed real enough to him. Dad moved out and I moved in. I was the enemy. So he was home and rebellious. He wanted his momma to get out of bed so bad he would act up just to get punished. It was a bitter scene with both of them yelling and her struggling out of bed chase him to his bedroom and paddle him with a wooden spoon.

His room was filled with thousands of toys as his mom used to have a daycare. Every toy had it's place and it overwhelmed him trying to clean up.

He once said he was scared of the toys. He also had a fascination and fear of the devil. His mother had indoctrinated him.

Once Ryan and my son were taking a bath together and they intentionally splashed most of the bath water on the floor. Ryan took a curtain rod and tried to gouge my son's eye out. His behavior was sometimes terrifying.

For three months we tried to keep everyone fed and clothed. And in the middle of that we sold dogs. Dog selling involved a shampoo, drying and brushing all the dogs that might be sold. While they were clean we kept them in the house. Some were potty trained, most were not.

People came by and bought dogs for bargain prices many having pity for Rhoda's delicate condition. Several sales were disastrous. One chihuahua died of a heart attack after less than one week in his new RV home. Another dog ran away in a field in town and the buyer wanted us to go find her for them, we couldn't and she was lost. A pair of dogs went to a family of 8 children and proved not house-broken. The busy exasperated mom yelled at me about it in the supermarket. I could only shrug and empathize.

The minister's wife had a carpet cleaning business and she came out with a crew of volunteers from the church and we moved all the furniture and deep cleaned the carpets with foam. Still Rhoda wanted certain dogs in the house and messes were made, which I cleaned up. One rickety old chihuahua really wanted to sleep with Rhoda and he left dried turds all over her bedroom. I insisted he go outside at night so he would hide from me and we would make a game of chase with yipes and nipping.

I did the shopping for food as well as trips to K-mart for wading pools and toys, always more things. She was on welfare and Medi-caid and had a way of acquiring things on sale. She had an urgent desire to get more things.

One day as I was stocking food I found In the freezer in the garage entombed in a styrofoam box a dead fetus wrapped in plastic. It bore the address of a laboratory and I wondered if it had been autopsied there. Perfectly formed, it had frost bitten toes and fingers and was curled up in the fetal position forever resting among the frozen foods. I understood her desire to keep it and I never talked to her about it. I figured that she would bury it when the right time came. It is so hard to let go.

In the last weeks of her pregnancy Rhoda developed gestational onset diabetes. Every food had to be measured or weighed and cooked carefully.

The visiting nurses came and went while I stayed to do the work. One praised me and I felt she wasn't seeing the whole imperfect picture.

Weekly I poop scooped the dog yards. One vicious sheltie named Ebony leaped up and bit me several times. There was a trick with the hose where I'd wave the hose in the air and the dogs would quiet down and run away. They disliked the cold water.

When it rained the dogs would huddle in the barn or in the dog houses but not Gizmo. Gizmo was the stud of the chihuahuas and he would look through the glass, soaking wet, lifting one paw then the other begging to be let in. I adored Gizmo and Rhoda saw this and gave him to me as a gift to reward me for caring for the dogs.

One afternoon I ironed in Rhoda's room and we watched a movie. Little Ryan came in and jammed the tape in the VCR and broke it. He didn't mean to, but it was a loss to all of us. No more movies.

Close to nine months I drove Rhoda to the hospital with labor pahins. She was sent home as it was not her time yet. One morning before dawn she came groaning across the house to awaken me and we rushed her to the hospital with little Ryan's babysitter meeting us in the labor room. We had an 18 mile drive to Bozeman and a slow truck would not let me pass. I got around him and escorted Rhoda into the hospital. The nurses were quite excited. They had seen the miscarriages.

One said, "Way to go Rhoda!" This time Rhoda was 10 centimeters dilated and soon gave birth to a healthy full term normal baby girl named Erin Rose.

I moved out as my job had ended, joyously. Her pregnancy had ended and she was no longer on bed rest. Also I had nothing left to give I was exhausted.

Chapter 35

Miss Peggy's Gentle Hands

Now when Mommy and Daddy go to work there is a special place I go. It is a warm room with colorful pictures on the walls. Miss Peggy cares for me until Mommy and Daddy get back. Miss Peggy's gentle hands hold me. I can rest on Miss Peggy's soft shoulder while she pat, pat, pats me on the back.

Miss Peggy reads me a book and we have music time in a circle. There is playtime on the playground she watches over me. Then there is quiet time and nap time when she rub, rub, rubs me on the back until I fall asleep. After snack time there is another circle time then Mommy and Daddy come to pick me up from daycare.

Bye Bye Miss Peggy! I'll see you tomorrow.

In the hospital there was a loving fish in the cancer wing. I named him the Empathy Fish and wrote the following highly fictionalized children's story about him:

Empathy Fish

There was a fish, not big nor small who lived in a large tank of other fish. What made this fish special and worthy of his own special story was that he cared. The Empathy Fish lived in a large tank in the center of a room in a children's hospital. In the tank full of fish, some were little like the neon tetras who darted about flashing their colors, some fish were beautiful like the graceful white angelfish, some fish were busy like the plecostomus that cleaned the sides of the tank with his big sucking lips and deep mouth.

There were all kinds of kids and their families who came to look at the fish tank. Just looking at the fish would bring them a little peace of mind and help them forget their pain and troubles.

Jean came to the hospital because she had leukemia, a kind of cancer. She was scared and tired that first day when she went for a walk down the hall with her mom to the fish tank. She watched the pretty white angelfish who swam back and forth admiring her own reflection on the glass. Then the Empathy fish swam forward and looked Jean in the eye. She watched as the Empathy Fish turned bright red.

Red is a strong color, the color of healthy blood and bone marrow. Jean liked the red color and the way the Empathy Fish moved his rubbery lips and blew bubbles at her. Later, when she had painful chemotherapy she remembered the red color and imagined her leukemia healing and her blood running red and strong again. Jean slowly began to get well. Every day, even if she felt tired and weak she wandered out to see the fish. The Empathy Fish turned bright red for her each time. The Empathy Fish made Jean feel special. "Thank you for being my friend." She murmured.

Emily had diabetes. She was getting used to having daily shots of insulin and checking her blood sugar. It made her feel mad. None of her friends had diabetes. It was unfair. She marched down the hall into the room where the big fish tank was. She forgot all about diabetes while she watched the fish. She pressed her face close to the tank to get a closer look. The pretty tetras swam by and the angelfish glided along.

The Empathy Fish swam over and looked into her eyes. He turned bright orange. The Empathy Fish turned the color of anger. Emily watched in amazement. It was as if the Empathy Fish knew exactly how she felt. Tears of relief fell down her cheeks and she sighed. Someone understood.   "You're the most beautiful fish of all." She said.

Every day with the medication Emily felt better. And every day she visited the Empathy Fish and he would look into her eyes and turn orange just for her.

John had a broken leg in a cast. He hobbled over to the fish tank on his new aluminum crutches. He admired all the fish as they swam about flashing their colors, being graceful and busily cleaning the sides of the tank. Then the Empathy Fish swam over and looked searchingly into John's eyes. Then the most amazing thing began to happen. The empathy fish turned bright yellow! Yellow was John's favorite color and it made him smile despite the pain from his broken leg.

"Thank you pretty fishy." John said. Later in his hospital bed when he had a hard time getting to sleep, he thought about the fish and the aching stopped and he fell into restful, healing sleep.

James had his appendix out. It left a very sore place on his tummy where there was a scar and black itchy stitches from the surgery. He leaned on his I.V. pole as he walked into the room where the fish tank was.

He watched the plecostomus cleaning the gravel by gathering it in his mouth, then spitting it out again. Then the Empathy Fish swam over and lined himself up to James' face. James looked into the Empathy Fish's eyes and slowly the Empathy Fish turned bright green.

"Wow, look at that fish." He thought.   James started to smile for the first time since his appendicitis. Green made him feel peaceful and loving. The color reminded him of summer days spent in the grass under the green apple tree in his grandparent's yard.

Amy had been in a scary car accident. She suffered bumps and bruises and whiplash, which is a very sore neck. She wore a funny looking neck brace which was embarrassing to her. The brace made her neck rigid and she could only look forward by turning her shoulders or turning her whole body around. This was very awkward.

When no one was in the hall she wandered out to the room where the fish tank was. She watched the fish for a long time. Then the Empathy Fish saw her. She moved closer to get a better look. He looked into her eyes and slowly turned blue. It was a bright shade of blue, like the sky on a cloudless day. Blue was just the color Amy felt inside, since the accident. She forgot about the neck brace.

"Fish don't notice things like that." She thought to herself with a sense of relief.

Dave had a bad cold that turned into pneumonia. The nurses and doctors gave him oxygen to help his breathing and antibiotics to kill the germs. When he was strong enough to walk he wandered the halls with his IV stand and his oxygen and found the room with the fish tank. He watched the neon tetras flit around and the white an-gelfish glide along. Then the empathy fish swam over and turned bright indigo as they looked into each other's eyes.

"What a wonderful fish you are," Dave said to the Empathy Fish.

Indigo was just the color Dave needed to see to feel better.

Bill had his tonsils out. His throat was very sore and he couldn't talk above a whisper. He was bored in his room so he went out to the room where the fish tank was. Bill watched the busy fish swimming in the tank. The Empathy Fish looked into his eyes and slowly turned violet. Violet was Bill's favorite color and it suited his subdued mood. He stared at the Empathy Fish for a long time.

"I don't need to talk to you. You understand just how I feel from my eyes." He thought.

One sunshiny day all the children came into the room where the empathy fish was waiting in his tank. He flipped over and slowly turned red, orange, yellow, green, blue, indigo and violet all of the colors of the rainbow. A rainbow is a symbol of hope. There was lots of hope for all the children. They saw the colors and began to talk to one another.

"He turned red for me." said Jean.

"He turned orange for me," said Emily.

"He turned yellow for me," said John.

"He turned green for me, said James.

"He turned blue for me, "said Amy.

"He turned indigo for me," said Dave.

"He turned violet for me," whispered Bill because his throat was sore from having his tonsils out.

And all the children, Jean, Emily, John, James, Amy, Dave and Bill watched as the Empathy Fish blew bubbles and flipped and swirled in the fish tank with his scales shining all the colors of the rainbow. For one magical moment the children forgot their pain and their braces, crutches, stitches and IV's and they held hands in a circle around the beautiful Empathy Fish in his tank, in the room of the children's hospital. And the children cared about each other as the Empathy Fish had cared about them.

Reality river and fish! A letter to provide civic duty public comment to the Fish Hatchery in Leavenworth.

Thank you for all your excellent information in the Draft Environmental Impact Statement # 01-18. My comments follow.

Throughout my whole childhood I played in the river and observed a wonderful ecosystem. In the old river were flora and fauna in abundance. I observed fish, beavers, raccoons, otters, bears, frogs and Great Blue Herons, eagles and gulls.

In the canal there were only a few species. The beavers determinedly chewed down cottonwoods but never succeeded in damming the canal. They built a dam on a bend in the old river.

As a concerned citizen I would be most interested in the gradual restoration of the old Icicle river as it provides superior riverine and wetland habitat.

Towards this end I suggest leaving the headgate dam to control water levels in the old river bed. The dam should be repaired if necessary to allow fish passage of Chinook Salmon, Steelhead and Bull Trout.

Structures 2, 3 and 4 should be demolished and removed. They could be removed during low water in an expedient manner that would minimize adverse impact on the river.

Structure 5 should be retained to block fish passage and meet fish hatchery and Native American fishing needs.

The area between structure 4 and dam 5 has sediment. If dredging is deemed necessary I hope it could be carefully planned out and done in a way that leaves most stream banks intact. What might seem destructive in the short term could have long term benefit. The riparian and wetland area is sensitive yet resilient over time. I suggest dredging in August when the water is low.

I am in support of the Native American tribal fishery and whatever sustains it. I also support the Fish Hatchery. Thank you for your excellent efforts in restoring this river. It is a beautiful place full of life.

Sincerely, Jennifer Telander Whitewing

Chapter 36

Meadow For Me
I want to dance in a meadow
I want to prance in the moss
with the scent of flowers
after rain showers
with tiny seeds
and pretty weeds
and colors all around
growing up from the ground
a little meadow
for little me
with colors and scents
wild and free
A meadow where I can swiftly go
feeling the grass between my toes

Mountain For Me
I want to climb a mountain
A mountain just my size
Not too steep and not too snowy
Not too stormy and not too blowy
3   A little mountain for little me
A mountain so I can see
Far and wide
Low and high
A mountain where I can touch the sky

I attended Bellevue Community College, Shoreline Community College in Seattle then transferred to The Evergreen State College in

Olympia.   My first year at Evergreen I was involuntarily committed to St Peter's hospital more times than I care to count or remember. It was hell on wheels with four point restraints and mind blurring body cramping muscle sore HALDOL shots. I still deeply hate Denny for orchestrating those involuntary hospitalizations.

FOREST FOR ME

I want to find a forest
A place to rest
        A place to see
        A grove of trees
        For little me
        A tall park
        With shadows dark
        Under a canopy of green
        A peaceful scene
        With wide roots
          And new shoots
          And mud squishing around my boots!

"You run hot and cold about going to Rocky Mountain College." My grandfather observed. I lasted one semester and five weeks. I took Chemistry, Anatomy and Physiology, Theater, Medical Termi-nology, Speech the first semester. Then I attempted to take Oil Painting, Chemistry, Ecology,   and Symphonic Band. I dropped out as a persona non grata and because my grades (a C average) weren't high enough to keep me competitive. Also I had the ballsy ovaries to complain about the program by posting broadsides on campus.

After RMC I worked four planting seasons for Volley Gayverts Nursery and also as a hotel maid for War Bonnet Inn. All part time and minimum wage!

I remember fondly my job at West Mont Home Management and Parkview Nursing home.

My grandmother was ill so Bry and I moved to Leavenworth to a comfy clean bright double wide trailer on Shore street. There we met the "Bratwurst of Love" A kindly basset hound. I worked at Sleeping Lady Mountain Resort. As a phone operator. We moved to Grandparent's home after 6 months on Shore street.

I did massage therapy part time and Bry got a security job with Art In The Park.In October Seth, I and kin trekked to the buggy Enchantment Lakes.

Seth told me, "Dr, Laura would want you to mother me rather than help granny." I inherited money when Jon my biological father died. We used it to uproot and relocate to Boise, Idaho. For the rest of Seth's school years I went to concerts, soccer games, band events and wrestling matches. I put a lot of miles on the ole COUNTRY SQUIRE FORD JALLOPY!

I slept in it several times. The back could fit a king sized mattress and the back seat was almost long enough to be comfortable. One night I was car camping or rather on the run from the law when I got locked out. I stumbled around in the snow and got hypothermia and near frostbite before I took a granite boulder and smashed out a passenger window so I could drive home. Very serious danger. I called Dr. Michael Karlfeldt for a house call. I almost had pneumonia.

Twelve years we have resided in Boise. I have worked hard. I worked at Serenity Retreat Therapeutic Spa, Fingerprints Nail Salon, Credit Union and Highland Springs Apartments.

We lived in a one bedroom creek side apartment then a cute cottage where I live with four cats.

I see Janet Strong NP for medication and Heather Tustison for art therapy and Brianna for guided meditations.

Life is beautiful although tragic. For example I lost money publishing my books Empathy Fish by Jen Telander Whitewing and Adventure Chalet by Peg Stark.

Seth's best friend from childhood got stabbed then died a few months later after undergoing intense medical treatment. God I miss Daniel. Lord I miss him so much.

I wish to do something fantastic. Something wonderful and loving and life bearing. Being loving to my son, husband and friends is part of it. Correspondence is part of it. I want to love. And in that love I want to spring forth a fountain of life.

I want to do something that will bring joy to many people. Something that will bring fame and good fortune. I want to write. I want to invent. I want to do more than I am now. It is good to strive and have hopes and dreams. It is the joy of living.

About the Author

Jennifer Jaye Millhouse White Unterseher Telander Whitewing lives in Boise Idaho in a home with three cats.

Jen does beadwork and writes and does massage therapy on occasion specializing in women.

www.ingramcontent.com/pod-product-compliance
Lightning Source LLC
Chambersburg PA
CBHW020507290526
45786CB00002B/515